BACTRIA

FROM THE EARLIEST TIMES TO THE EXTINCTION OF BACTRIO-GREEK RULE IN THE PUNJAB.

BACTRIA

FROM THE EARLIEST TIMES TO THE EXTINCTION OF BACTRIO-GREEK RULE IN THE PUNJAB.

(*Being the Hare University Prize Essay, 1908*)

BY

H. G. RAWLINSON, M.A., I.E.S.

Professor of English, Deccan College, Poona; Late Scholar, Emmanuel College, Cambridge.

GYAN

Published by

GYAN

Gyan Publishing House
5, Ansari Road
Daryaganj, New Delhi-110002
Phone: 011-47034999, 9811692060
E-mail: books@gyanbooks.com

Distribution Network
gyanbooks.com
India, USA, Canada, UK, Australia, France

ISBN : 978-81-212-2770-4 (HB)
First Published, 1909

2nd Impression 2021

Printed at: Gyan Press, Delhi.

Bactria
Author: H. G. Rawlinson

BACTRIA

FROM THE EARLIEST TIMES TO THE EXTINCTION OF BACTRIO-GREEK RULE IN THE PUNJAB.

(Being the Hare University Prize Essay, 1908.)

BY

H. G. RAWLINSON, M.A., I.E.S.,

Professor of English, Deccan College, Poona; Late Scholar, Emmanuel College, Cambridge.

Bombay:
THE "TIMES OF INDIA" OFFICE.
1909.

To The Memory

of

JAMES ADAM, Litt. D.,

Late Senior Fellow and Tutor, Emmanuel College, Cambridge,

THIS ESSAY

IS AFFECTIONATELY DEDICATED

BY

THE AUTHOR.

स्मरणार्थम्.

"If through the Bactrian Empire European ideas were transmitted to the Far East, through that and other similar channels Asiatic ideas found their way to Europe."

BUCKLE, *Intellectual Development of Europe*, I. ii.

PREFACE.

THE primary interest of Bactria must always rest upon the fact that it was the great connecting link between East and West. The time has, let us hope, passed, when scholars can rest content with regarding the two great civilizations, Hellenic and Hindu, which the Aryan race has produced, as things apart. Each has probably played an essential part in the development of the other. Greek Philosophy from Plato to the Gnostics shows Eastern influence, as clearly as Indian art, drama, and astronomy bear traces of contact with the West. In the Bactrio-Indian civilization of the Punjab, we are enabled to study the fusion of the two races at the point of contact.

The history of Bactria has besides an interest in itself; it is the story of a little-known and adventurous race, who show many elements of true greatness. To the important Parsi community, who may possibly be themselves the descendants, to some degree, of the Bactrian Greeks, the story of the historic capital of Bactria, the ancient cradle of the creed of Zarathustra, and full of memories of the great Iranian race, should prove to be not without interest.

I must gratefully acknowledge my indebtedness to Professor E. T. Rapson for the valuable advice he has so often given me on difficult points, and for his unfailing interest and sympathy.

H. G. RAWLINSON.

Poona, 1909.

INTRODUCTION.

THE great Bactrian Kingdom, lying on the extreme flank of the Persian, and later the Seleucid, Empire has an interest, all its own, to the student of Ancient History. It was here that the East merged into the West, and the West eventually overflowed its bounds and encroached upon the Eastern world, producing a wonderful cosmopolitan civilization, the history of which it is the object of this essay to investigate.

Many circumstances concurred to give to Bactria a position of unique importance in the Ancient World. It was the grand "clearing-house" of the world's commerce; the three roads which met at Bactria, brought together caravans from the Khyber, from China, and from the great trade-route which linked up Asia with Europe, and, running north of the Hyrcanian desert, tapped the chief colonial trading centres of the Levant.

Besides this, Bactria was immensely fertile, and had a considerable trade of her own; the twelfth satrapy of the Persian Empire, paying three hundred and sixty talents yearly into the Imperial Treasury, she was respected both for her wealth and for many other reasons.

Bactria, "the pride of Iran", was looked upon as the heart of the Empire, the cradle of the national religion. The fierce independent Iranian nobles of the Bactria were celebrated for their prowess as cavalrymen, and for the tenacity with which they clung to their national customs. Later, Bactria became of importance to the Seleucid Empire, as, to some extent, it had been to Persia, as the barrier-state which kept watch and ward over the Scythians of the Northern Steppes. In this respect it failed; partly owing to the rivalry of Parthia, partly to the ambitions imperial policy of the Bactrian monarchs, which exhausted the population while it extended their territories, the Bactrian Greeks were forced to evacuate their northern home on the Oxus, and to enact the last act of the drama of Greek occupation of the East, in the Kabul and Punjab. The history of Bactria is the history of the absorption of a race, but not before it presents results which are of considerable historical importance. It seemed indeed as if Bactria was at one time likely to occupy the position which Parthia afterwards assumed in Asia Minor; but the healthy and supremely national civilization of the latter country quickly eclipsed the brilliant but exotic product of Greek invasion, which for a time threatened its existence. The political 'centre of gravity' of Bactria tended steadily to move southwards and eastwards, till finally the Greek element was entirely absorbed into India.

The early history of the Iranian settlement of Bactria is completely lost in a mist of fable and legend. Only two statements appear to have any historical importance, the unanimous agreement of historians that Zoroaster was a Bactrian, and Justin's assertion that Bactria "was founded by the Scythians", the significance of which I have endeavoured to point out.

With the annexation of Bactria by the Persian Empire, we come upon surer ground, and Herodotus gives us a good deal of information about this important satrapy. I have quoted from Rawlinson's Edition (1867), and also from that Editor's transcription of the Behistun Inscription, with the interesting allusion to Dardases, the satrap employed by Darius to put down the revolt of Phraortes of Margiana.

Bactria next becomes prominent in history during Alexander's Campaign ; for his operations against those stubborn horsemen, and his subsequent operations in India, we chiefly depend upon Arrian's *Anabasis*, and the work of Quintus Curtius " *De Rebus Gestis Alexandri Magni* ". The latter has perhaps been under-estimated ; he based his work to a great extent on the rhetorician Cleitarchus, a notoriously untrustworthy authority, who was accused, on one occasion at least, of eking out history with a dash of romance. On the other hand, Curtius corrects Cleitarchus in at least one instance (IX, 11, 21), and though he has been blamed for ignorance of geography, tactics and astronomy, he preserves many details of the campaigns which Arrian omits. Arrian is, on the whole, however, immensely superior as a source of accurate information, his account being based on the official records of Ptolemy and Aristobulus, who seems to have resisted the temptations to which Cleitarchus succumbed. Arrian, however, omits (perhaps intentionally) one episode, the cruel treatment of the Branchiadae ; and in one instance he is less clear, as far as geography is concerned, than Curtius ; he is very confused and vague about the position the town of Zariaspa, which he seems to place in Sogdia. The edition of Curtius here quoted is that of T. Davison (1826).

Mention must be made, " *honoris causa* " of that admirable work of Strabo, " *the Geography* ", which is a mine of accurate information, not only on Bactria, but on the surrounding tribes ; the full significance of a good deal that Strabo records is still awaiting recognition. I have cited Falconer's translation (Bohn 1856).

Besides innumerable references in the fragments of Ctesias, in Polybius in the Periplus (for which I have used Mr. McCrindle's Translation), in the Minor Greek Geographical Writers, (Muller 1847) ; in Appian ; Diodorus Siculus ;

Plutarch ; Clement of Alexandria ; and such late writers as John of Malala and Saint Isodore of Charax (all of which often throw unexpected light upon obscure points,) we have Justin's "*Trogi Pompei Historiarum Phillipicarum Epitoma*". If we accept the incidental references in Strabo, Justin is our only continuous authority for the history of Bactria after the revolt of Diodotus. Justin, after a quite disproportionate popularity in the middle ages, has now sunk into a state of perpaps unmerited neglect. Justin has neither the accuracy of Arrian nor the graces of Curtius, and has received many shrewd knocks of recent years. "Trogus was a sad historian, or Justin a vile abridger", is the remark of an eighteenth century translator, "but as we have the testimony of many famous men in favour of Trogus, Justin will stand condemned". It must be remembered that Justin wrote, as Adolf Holm puts it, "for a circulating library public", and not for scholars, and we should be grateful to him for the immense mass of information, which would have been otherwise lost, carelessly though it is handed down. It is obviously impossible, as some critics would have us do, to mistrust every piece of information uncorroborated by further testimony, though where Justin is in opposition to other authorities, he may be safely disregarded. The modern editor has treated Justin with scant courtesy ; the edition here quoted is that by Wetzel (1823).*

The Chinese authorities who give a detailed account of the movements of the Scythian tribes which resulted in the overthrow of Bactria, are obviously inaccessible to the ordinary scholar, who has to depend upon the results of expert investigation.

* Since writing the above, I have obtained the admirable French edition, (translation, text and notes,) published by Garnier Frères. The introduction is an exhaustive and very impartial summary of Justin's merits and faults.

This question has been dealt with in various detached articles in English and foreign periodicals, among which I may mention Mr. V. A. Smith's articles on the "Sakas in Northern India", in the *Zeitschrift der Deutschen Morgenlandischen Gesellschaft* 1907 (II. p. 402); and the articles which have appeared in the *Journals of the Royal Asiatic Society*, from the pens of Dr. Fleet and Mr. F. W. Thomas (1905, p. 657, 1906, pp. 181, 211, 460, &c.,) and numerous contributions to the Bengal and Bombay Branches' Magazines, which are referred to in detail. The latest contributions to the subject are M. Chavanne's "*Turcs Occidentaux*" and "*Le Voyage de Song Yun*", and the articles appearing from the pen of M. Sylvain Levi in the *Journal Asiatique*. The most important of all, however, is Dr. Otto Franke's "*Beitrage aus chineseschen Quellen zur Kenntris der Turkovolker and Skythen Zentralasiens*" (Berlin 1904), which effectually supersedes former works on the subject.

Of modern works on the subject of Bactria, the first noticeable book was from the pen of *Bayer* (St. Petersburg 1738). An even earlier contribution to the subject is "*The modern History of Hindoostan, comprehending that of the Greek Empire of Bactria and other great Asiatic Kingdoms bordering on its Western Frontier*", by Thomas Maurice (1802), a rare book, and of antiquarian interest only.

The first real contribution to the scientific study of the history of that country, however, is H. H. Wilson's *Ariana Antiqua* (London 1841), a magnificent work in every way, embodying the results of Massom's researches. It is natural that after sixty years a good many of Wilson's theories are now definitely disproved, but the indebtedness of all subsequent scholars to this great pioneer in this department of historical research is incalculable.

Of later works, Rawlinson's "*Sixth Oriental Monarchy*" deals at some length with the history of Parthia, Bactria's great rival for supremacy in the 2nd century B. C.; and Spiegel's "*Eranische Alterthumer*" has been consulted (Leipsic 1878). For the history of the Seloucid Empire, Mr. E. R. Bevan's "*House of Seleucus*" is the latest and most exhaustive authority. It contains many invaluable references to Bactria.

But the most useful contributions towards the study of Bactrian history are perhaps those from the pen of Professor A. Von Gutschmid of Tubingen; his *Geschichte Irans*, and his article contributed to the *Encyclopædia Britannica*, (ninth edition) under the heading "*Persia*", (section two), have proved of great service. The former has been described as "a highly condensed but most informing work. It abounds in brilliant, if over bold conjectures". (*W. Wroth. Cat. Parthian coins in B. M.*) Some of these are noticed and corrected in notes to this Essay; perhaps one of most valuable features of the latter is the excellent bibliography and criticism of authorities at the end. In the recent volume of Mr. V. A. Smith, on the "*Early History of India*", (Oxford, 1904), the whole question of Bactrian history is briefly but thoroughly dealt with. This volume has been freely used and my indebtedness is acknowledged in my notes.

On general questions, reference has been made to a great number of works, those of Grote, Adolf, Holm, and Professor Bury in particular; to M. Babelon's *Rois de Syria*; to Lassen's "*Indische Alterthums-Kunde*"; and to Sir W. W. *Hunter's Imperial Gazeteer of India* (1881), of which Vol. IV. has been particularly full of information.

Mention must be made, also, to the "*Sacred Books of the East*", edited by Max Muller. Vol. XXX—VI, containing the "*Questions of King Milinda*", with Introductory remarks by Mr. Rhys Davids, have been constantly referred to: other volumes are mentioned in the notes wherever they were used. I have already referred to J. W. Mc.Crindle's translation of the "*Periplus Maris Erythraei*"; other works from the same pen have been used with profit, especially his "*Ancient India as described by Megasthenes and Arrian*" (1877).

The history of Bactria is illustrated and supplemented by the magnificent coins which have been from time to time discovered in great quantities, and, in many cases, in an excellent state of preservation. Many of the Indo-Bactrian monarchs are only known to us by their coins, and the arrangements of these in chronological order is a task still occupying the attention of numismatists. I have not attempted to put forward any new theory on this subject, which awaits really fresh information; *adhuc sub judice list est.*

Besides the older work of Wilson and Van Prinsep, much of which is now out of date, an exhaustive list of the Bactrian and Seleucid coins in the British Museum will be found in Professor Gardner's *Catalogue of the coins of Greek and Scythic Kings of Bactria and India in the British Museum*, which has been referred to extensively in illustration of this essay. The same author has issued a catalogue of the coins of the Seleucid Kings, which has occasionally proved of assistance. Both these volumes contain valuable introductions. The Parthian coins in the British Museum have been catalogued by Warwick Wroth. A very important work by Mr. V. A. Smith, "*A Catalogue of the coins in the Calcutta Museum*", is now being issued. The first volume has been of the utmost use in supplementing the work of Gardner. Other volumes which have been freely consulted are Von Sallet's "*Die Nachfolger Alexander des grossen im Baktrien*" (Berlin 1878), and General Sir Alexander Cunningham's "*Coins of Ancient India*" and "*Coins of Alexander's successors in the East*" in the *Numismatic Chronicle* (68—73).

Professor E. J. Rapson has contributed a short resume of the latest conclusions he has arrived at, on the vexed questions of Indo-Bactrian coinage, to the *Gundriss der Indo-arischen* Philologie, which I have consulted with profit.

There are no Graeco-Bactrian inscriptions extant. For Indian inscriptions bearing on the subject, I have used Buhler's "*Epigraphia Indica*".

The vexed question, as to the influence which the inruption of the Bactrian Greeks had upon the progress of civilization in India, has been dealt with from two opposite points of view. Niese, on the one hand, holds that the whole subsequent development of India was due to Alexander's influence. On the other hand, Mr. V. A. Smith, who says that Niese's "astonishing paradox" is "not supported by a single fact", considers that Alexander's invasion taught India nothing, and that the great Imperial ideas of the Maurya monarchs were Persian, if anything at all, save a natural and indigenous political development.

The indebtedness of India to the West in astronomy, art and drama, has been touched upon by Sir W. W. Hunter in Vol. IV of *the Imperial Gazetteer of India* (London 1881), p. 261; but the real question, whether the Western influence here to be discerned, is really due to the Bactrian Greeks, who had once held sway in the Punjab or to Graeco-Roman sources has only been adequately dealt with by recent writers. I have tried to point out in this essay, that, while in astronomy the influence of Western thought appears to have been felt comparatively late, in art we must distinguish between the cosmopolitan characteristics of the "Indo-Corinthian" architecture, which are clearly more Roman than Greek, and the singular purity of the Gandhara bas-reliefs, which have a purely Hellenic air.

The older books on Indian Architecture have been of little use on this point; important modern contributions to the study of Graeco-Indian art, are the *Catalogue of the Archæological Collections in the Indian Museum, Calcutta*, by Dr. J. Anderson (1883), and Mr. V. A. Smith's most able paper (J.A.S.B., 1889, Vol. 58, i, p. 115.) on "*Graeco-Roman Influence on the Civilization of Ancient India*". Mr. Growse's "*Mathura*", and General Sir Alexander Cunningham's extensive "*Reports of the Archælogical Survey of India*", must not escape notice; the latter, of course, is invaluable.

Most important of all, however, are the admirable contributions of M. A. Foucher, who has investigated the Peshawar district under the auspices of the Academie des Inscriptions et Belles Lettres. Of M. Foucher's works, the following have been consulted:—"*Notes sur la geographie ancienne du Gandhara*" (Hanoi 1902), "*Sur la Frontiere Indo-Afghane*" (Paris 1901), and his recent "*L'art du Ghandhara*", of which only Vol. I. has been available to me. It is with great reluctance that we are forced to put forward the date of the famous sculptures of the Gandhara district and ascribe them to the period of the Kushan and Scythic monarchs. Foucher's admirable remarks may be of some consolation to the student of history, who contemplates ruefully the ruin of shattered theories: "Nous en attribuerions volontiers la paternité à ces artistes errants qui colportaint alors dans les provinces, et jusque par délà les bornes de l'Empire, les procédés déjà stereotypés de l'art Grec. Les sculpteurs qui pour le benefice des pieux donateurs dû Gandhâra, adaptèrent le type d'Apollon à la représentation des divinités boudhiques, semblent bien les petits-cousins de ceux qui, vers la même époque, coiffaient le Mithra persan du bonnet Ghrygien de Ganymède . . . et donnaient au Jésus des Catacombes les traits d'Orphée ou du Bon Pasteur."

Addenda.—Mention must be made of Dr. Stein's "*Sand-buried ruins of Khotan*" (1903), which seems to show that, under Kanishka, Graeco-Buddhist culture spread far into the Khotan deserts, following in the wake of Indian arms.

An important article by W. W. Tarn in the *Journal of the Hellenic Society*, 1902, entitled "*Notes on Hellenism in Bactria and India*" has been consulted and found to be of great assistance.

On the subject of *Indian Sculpture and Painting*, Mr. E. B. Havell's book (Murray 1908) is the latest authority. Mr. Havell repudiates with vigour the idea that Indian art owes anything to Graeco-Roman influence [see the Review in the R.A.S. Journal April, 1909, [p. 541 *ff*].

CHAPTER I.

Bactria, its Geography and Resources.

"Vires Orientis et ultima Bactra."

THAT portion of ancient Iran, known to Greek writers as the province of Bactria,[1] was usually considered to include the strip of country lying between the slopes of the Hindu-Kush and the river Oxus. To the north of it lay the kindred province of Sogdiana, which is intimately connected by its position, nationality, and history with Bactria, and will be considered at the same time.[2] Sogdiana stretched north to the banks of the Jaxartes, and may be roughly defined as the strip of country lying between the two rivers. To the north and east, over the river, lay the illimitable Scythian steppes, even now fraught with vague terrors to the inhabitants of the Oxus Valley, on account of the restless hordes of nomads, ever menacing the frontier.

---

1 Origin uncertain. Perhaps from (A) paktra—"Northern" in Zend, it being the most northerly of the four primitive Aryan settlements.

2 See Strabo (or Erathosthenes) XI, 8. 1. ff.

Bactria was looked on by the Persian monarchs as the heart of Iran. "It was the boast of all Ariana",[1] says Strabo, and it owed its importance to the concurrence of many circumstances. It lay directly in the great trade route to India: the caravans, then as now, passed through Kabul and Kandahar on their way from India to the Caspian and Asiatic ports; and, strategically, Bactria was of paramount importance as a frontier state, guarding the immense empire of the Medes on its weakest flanks.[2] Besides, Bactria had a considerable trade of its own. It produced all the Greek articles of food except the olive[3]. Silphium grew in great quantities on the slopes of the Hindu-Kush, and formed a valuable article of commerce in itself, besides proving of use in the fattening of an excellent breed of sheep[4]; and Bactrian horses were as famous as the Arabs of a later day[5]. Quintus Curtius[6] sums up the chief geographical character-

---

1 Strabo XI. 11. 1. cf. Virgil Georgics II. 137.

"Sed neque Medorum silvæ ditissima terra
Laudibus Italiæ certet, non Bactra neque Indi"

for the almost proverbial fertility of the country. It paid the Great King 360 talents tribute—a very respectable sum, attesting to the richness of the soil; far short, however, of Assyria (the richest province) with 1,000 talents (*vide* Herodotus III, 92).

2 See the Behistun Inscription, Col. 3., para. 3. On the rebellion of Phraortes in Margiana, Darius sent one Dadarses to "Smite the people that owned him not.——And by God's grace, he defeated the rebels".

3 Strabo. XI., 11. 1.

4 Arrian. Anab: 3. 29.

5 The "Medic herb" (lucerne) grew all over Iran and made admirable fodder.

6 Q. Curtius. VII. 4. 26 (18).

istics of the country in an excellent manner:—"The soil of Bactria," he remarks, "varies considerably in its nature. In some spots extensive orchards and vineyards produce abundant fruit of a most delicious quality. The soil there is rich and well-watered. The warmer parts produce crops of corn: the rest is better for pasture land. The fertile portions are densely populated, and rear an incredible number of horses." This description has been cordially endorsed by one of the most distinguished of the early explorers of modern Turkestan[1].

We may compare whata more recent visitor has to say on the subject. The "Times" correspondent with Sir Peter Lumsden's force, writing on March 12th, 1882, says :—"Two branches of the Parapamisus run from Herat to the Hari Rud[2]. The south branch of the Parapamisus is represented by gentle undulations of gravelly soil, covered with camel thorn and assafœdita[3], which intervene between Herat and the frontier . . . . . ." "Groves of pistachio and mulberry trees, bushes, wild carrots testified to the richness of the soil, irrigated in many places by streams of the purest water alive with fish."

1 Sir A. Burnes (Journey to Bokhara. I. 245) remarks that "The language of the most graphic writer could not delineate this country with greater exactness."

2 The classical "Arius".

3 This tallies in a remarkable way with Arrian. Anab. 3, 29.

Curtius, however, is careful to point out that his description only applies to the fertile alluvial soil of the Oxus valley, and the slopes of the Parapamisus. Vast tracts, he continues, consist of barren sand-dunes, and when the wind blows from the north-west, every land-mark is obliterated. Hills of sand are piled up in every direction, and the whole face of the country is so altered, that the traveller can only steer his course by the stars. One curious effect of this is noticed by Arrian and Strabo[1]. Many of the rivers, like the Arius (Hari Rud)[2], the so-called Polytimetus[3] in Sogdiana (the name is a corruption, Strabo says, of the local word, coined by the Macedonians and afterwards sanctioned by Aristobulus), flow into the sand and are absorbed. This is particularly noticeable in the case of the Hari Rud, which disappears near the oasis of Tejend, in the Turcoman sands. It is, no doubt, owing to some exaggerated story arising from this phenomenon that Curtius has such a strange tale to tell of the Polytimetus[4]. "This river," he gravely asserts, "is confined between

[1] Strabo. Geog: XI. 5. of Arrian. Anab. IV. 6.
[2] The classical "Arius".
[3] The modern "Zarafshan", *i.e.*, "bringing down gold"—like the Pactolus. No doubt the ancient name (whatever it may have been) referred, like the modern one, to its auriferous qualities, and the Greek "Polytimetus" was a sort of rough equivalent for the Iranian word, whatever that was.
[4] Q. C. VII. 10. 1.

narrow banks and suddenly plunges into the bowels of the earth. The sound of flowing water enables one to trace its subterranean course; though the ground above, in spite of the volume of water flowing underneath, shows no traces of moisture." The phenomenon may be also observed in Khotan, where rivers have even completely changed their course[1]. Matthew Arnold's description of the Oxus inevitably rises to the mind in this connection :—

> "Then sands begin
> To hem his watery course, and dam his streams
> And split his currents, that for many a league
> The shorn and parcelled Oxus strains along
> Through beds of sand and matted rushy isles."

It should be added that Sogdiana was far less fertile than Bactria. Here the deserts predominated, the only really fertile country being in the vicinity of the royal city of Maracanda. These deserts had a certain protective value to Bactria and Sogdiana: they presented to the invader an obstacle which it has puzzled many a general to surmount from Alexander to Skobeleff and Kuropatkin.

But the most characteristic geographical feature of Bactria has yet to be mentioned. I refer to the

---

1 The Oxus in Strabo's days flowed into the Caspian, near Krasnovodsk. The rivers in the Punjab have evidently altered considerably, to the vexation of the historian of Alexander's operations in the East. The modern Balkh is some miles from the river (the ancient Bactrus) on which it seems once to have stood. For Khotan, see Dr. Stein's recent book, *Passim*.

rock fortresses scattered throughout the country, which nature and human art in many cases made well nigh impregnable, strong enough, at any rate, to tax all the resources of 'the great Emathian conqueror' himself. Strabo[1] gives us a minute account of these, as they existed in the days of the Macedonian invasion. The chief of them was the citadel of Sisimithres, which was surrendered by Oxyartes to Alexander. It was said to have been fifteen stadia high and eighty stadia in circumference at the base. The summit formed a broad plateau, capable of containing a garrison of five hundred men and susceptible of cultivation[2]. Maracanda in Sogdiana, the city of the Sogdian princes, was said to have been double this in height: on the Acropolis stood the royal palace, the scene, probably, of the tragedy which cost Clitus his life. In mediæval times it became famous in history and legend under the name of Samarkhand[3]. But the strongest and in many ways the most remarkable of these cities was the capital of the province of Bactria, Bactra or Zariaspa, "the city of the horse," as the Iranians

---

1 *Vide* XI. 88. 4, &c.

2 The most remarkable specimen was the gigantic citadel of Aornos, apparently the Mahaban Hill. See V. Smith. Early History of India. p. 68 (p. 71 Second Edition). The traveller will be reminded of the magnificent Si-giriya (Lion's rock) in Ceylon, where Kasappa held out for fifteen years, and of the great forts characteristic of the Deccan country.

3 I venture to assume the identity of Bactra and Maracanda with Balkh and Samarcand respectively.

loved to call it, a fitting name for the chief town of a land famous for its gallant cavalry. Its strength is attested to by Polybius,[1] who speaks of the heroic resistance it made on one occasion, so that the 'siege of Bactra,' was reckoned among the most remarkable feats of arms in ancient military history, and had long become a common place for the rhetorician and poet. Onesicritus[2] does not give a very favourable account of it, it is true. "The suburbs," he says, "are clean, but the interior is full of bones, as the old and sick are given to dogs to devour: these animals," he adds, "are known as 'Entombers' by the inhabitants."

Onesicritus, however, may be repeating a story which arose from the Zoroastrian custom of exposing their dead on "towers of silence." The Greeks looked on this 'barbarous' habit with a not unnatural repugnance. Alexander, we are told, abolished the practice,[3] as the English have abolished 'Sati' in India; and the story of the part played by the dogs may be traced to the custom still practised

---

1 Polybius XXIX. 12. 8. *Probably* by Antiochus the Great, but we cannot be *certain* (Von. Gutschmidt apparently is). Polybius does not say so.

2 Apud Strabonem. XI, 11, 3.

3 For the general persecution of the Ignicolists by Alexander (see Rehatsek's article on the "Alexander Myth." J. B. R. A. S. XV. 1867).

Nizam records that Alexander burnt the Avesta books and forbade fire-worship.

by the Parsis, of showing the body of a newly-dead person to a dog, for the purpose of keeping off the evil spirit lying in wait for the soul of the departed. In the city of Bactria stood a shrine and statue of the great goddess Anaitis,[1] or (to give her her Iranian name) Anahid, one of the most revered of the deities of Iran and the surrounding nations, and worshipped under various names throughout Asia Minor, particularly in Armenia. Whether she was connected with the goddess known to us by the name of "Diana of the Ephesians" is uncertain. Both alike were identified with Greek Artemis, and the extreme license prevailing at her

---

1 *Anahid or Anaitis.* This goddess was also known as Nanea or Anea, and as such is referred to in the Apocrypha Mac : II. 1, 13. Her shrines were very rich, and more than once were plundered by Seleucid or Parthian to replenish their coffers,—Mithridates I was guilty of this offence. (Antiochus Epiphanes in Elymais (Mac : I. 6, 13) was another. Cf. Rawlinson's Sixth Oriental Monarchy p. 73.)

Sir J. G. Wilkinson identifies her with Venus; he says the modern Persian name for Venus is Anahid. This view is supported by the accounts of prostitution at her temple in Acilisene (this is not, of course, conclusive) mentioned by Strabo. XI, 14, 16—(see Rawlinson's Herodotus, Appendix to Book III, Essay I).

She is also perhaps the Mylitta or Alitta of Babylon (Rawlinson Herod. I, 131.) See an article by Sykes, in Transactions, Bombay J. R. A. S. III. p. 281. "The angel corresponding to Alitta is the Persian Anahita. The Iranian deity who would remind us of the Ling and the Yoni, would be *Anahita, who is the personification of the fructifying powers of Nature.*" (Sakti.) See especially what is said by Hunter, Imperial Gazetteer IV., p. 303, "India," 1881, on the Sakta sects, non-Aryan in origin.*

*For Dubois, see translation by Beauchamp, Clarendon Press, 1897, (Mœurs Institutions, et ceremonies des Peuples de l' Inde, par J. A. Dubois). He is only valuable as describing India as he found it; his general statements are untrustworthy. For the Sakti Puja see II., Ch. IX. *Passim.*

festivals tempts the student of comparative mythology to see in both the Hindu goddess Sakti. Sakti, like the Ephesian Artemis, is the goddess of fecundity, and her feasts, the 'Sakti Puja,' described by that remarkable student of Indian customs, the Abbe Dubois, are strikingly like the 'Bacchanalian' feast called the "Sacæa", celebrated at Zela, in which men and women 'passed day and night in lascivious indulgence."[1] This feast is said to have been instituted by Cyrus in commemoration of his victory over the Sacae; but it was probably a national præ-Aryan feast of Anahid, and anterior to the Persian victory it was said to commemorate. The feast, Strabo tells us, took place "wherever there was a temple of this goddess," and he adds the significant detail, that the celebrants were "dressed in Scythian raiment."

We are fortunate in possessing further details with regard to the Bactrian Anahid. She is invoked in the Zend-Avesta as the "High-girdled one, clad in a golden mantle. On thine head is a golden crown, with eight rays and an hundred stars: thou art clad in a robe of thirty otter skins, of the sort with shining fur"[2]. That this actually

1 Strabo. XI, 8, 4, also 6, and see what he says in 11, 16.

Vol. II, p. 28. "Sacred Books of the East," Darmesteter's translation.

describes the statue in Bactria is almost conclusively proved by a fine coin of Demetrius[1] representing a goddess whose appearance answers almost exactly to the description here quoted; and our doubts are still further set at rest by a reference in Clement of Alexandria to a 'statue of Anaitis at Bactria'[2].

Such was the great city of Bactra, standing on the high Road between east and west, a 'meeting place of the nations': situated in the midst of the fertile foothills of the Parapamisus, with its almost impregnable Acropolis and its famous shrine, it was a fit place for the confluence of the two civilizations. The modern traveller finds no remains of its ancient glories in the rambling town of modern Balkh: all traces of the old Iranian and Greek cities are hidden under a mass of mediæval Mahommedan ruins[3].

It is perhaps necessary to add a few words on the identity of Bactra and Zariaspa. Some modern authorities still consider that the two names

---

1 Gardner's "Coins of the Greek and Scythic, Kings of Bactria and India, in the British Museum." Plate III. 1. Perhaps she appears in the coin of Euthydemus figured by W. Wilson, Ariana Antiqua. Plate II, 1. (Wilson says it is Apollo, however !)

2 Protrepticos, Ch. 65. He calls it Aphrodite Tanais: but his meaning seems clear. (? Tanais, a corruption of Anaitis.)

3 Bactria was one of the capitals of the great Hun Emperors, and must have been built over by 500 A. D. with fresh materials. General Ferrier (*Caravan Journeys* p. 206) is impressed with the size of the ruins. But he refers to Mediæval, not ancient, remains. However, he appears to have seen some inscribed bricks among them. See Encycl: (Brit: 9th Edition) sub voce "Turkestan".

represent entirely different towns. Strabo[1] expressly states that Bactra was the capital. The name Bactra, he says, was connected with the river Bactrus, a tributary of the Oxus, which flows through it. The probable explanation is that which Pliny[2] hints at ("Oppidum Zariaspa, quod *postea* Bactra a flumine appellatum est")—that Bactra was a later (Greek) name which gradually superseded the older (Iranian) one. Quintus Curtius seems to know the city only by its later title. In this connection it is not without interest to notice an early conjecture of La Rochette's, by which Zariaspa is connected with Zara, the Persian Artenis, possibly Anahid herself[3].

On the other hand, Ptolemy seems to distinguish the two, and he is apparently followed by Arrian. Arrian does not explicitly state that Zariaspa is in Sogdia, but he seems to imply it[4]. On one occasion specially he is describing Alexander's reduction of Sogdia, and goes on to say that he wintered in Zariaspa. Zariaspa is made the temporary capital, where Alexander receives Phraataphernes and Stasanor, and where the murder of Clitus takes place.

---

1 Strabo., XI., 11, 3.
N. H., VI, 18.
3 Wilson "Ariana." p. 297.
4 Anab. IV, 7, 1.

In the story as given by Curtius, these events happened at Maracanda. As Maracanda was the royal capital, this seems far more probable, and we can merely conclude that Arrian has blundered. Zariaspa being spoken of as *a* 'capital', he has come to the conclusion that it must be *the* capital of Sogdia.[1]

1 *Bactra and Zariaspa.*—Arrian is supported by some modern authorities. See Adolf Holm's Greek History (English Translation) Vol. 1. Ch. 26, Note 1. Bury in his Greek History (following apparently Von Schwarz's "Alexander des Grosson Felzuge im Turkestan") says that Zariaspa and Bactra bore somewhat the same relation to one another as the Sogdian cities of Maracanda and Sogdiana. He identifies Zariaspa with the modern Chargui, on the Oxus, a good deal to the N-W. of Bactria. (p. 791, and the accompanying map.)

CHAPTER II.

THE EARLY HISTORY OF BACTRIA.

THE Bactrian Empire was founded by the Scythians, says Justin[1]. This statement probably comes very near the truth; for, by examining the scattered notices in Justin, Curtius, Arrian and Strabo[2], we shall find there are ample traces of a non-Aryan helot population existing in Bactria up to the time of Alexander; it would appear highly probable that we are here presented with a condition of things quite similar to that which obtained in ancient Sparta or early Norman England, unless an even closer parallel is to be found in the oligarchies of ancient Thessaly.

We know that there was a constant tendency on the part of the tribes beyond the Jaxartes to move south: this tendency was part of the wave-

---

[1] Justin II. 3.

[2] Especially Strabo. XI. 8 4 "The Sacae used to make raids like the Cimmerians.......*They occupied Bactria*". Herodotus refers to the Sacae and Bactrians in one breath, constantly, as if there were but little difference between them; as, indeed, there would be, if the Satrapy of Bactria consisted of Sacae with an Iranian aristocracy.

See especially the story of Masistes. (IX. 113.) Masistes would have stirred up a revolt, had he gone back to *Bactria among the Sacae.*

Hystaspes (VII. 54) was in command of the "*Bactrians and Sacae*".

movement which has produced the great invasions of the west from time immemorial[1], and it is likely that the fertile Oxus valley was already in possession of Scythian tribes,—Sacae very probably[2], when the Iranians appeared. Many of the customs which we look upon as purely as "Zoroastrian", may be really of non-Aryan origin[3]. The practice of exposing the dead appears to have been common in various forms among many Scythian tribes. Can it be possible that the practice merely received a sanction from the religion of Zoroaster? We may compare the accounts of the Bactrian customs with regard to the dead and infirm, with those obtaining among the Parthians, Derbices, the Cei[4]; the Caspii[5] and the Massegetae[6], from which it may be inferred that they all had a common origin, and that præ-Aryan, and possibly Scythian or 'Sacæn'.

---

1 It has been suggested that in the Sacae we find the earliest mention of the Turk. (Bury, History of Greece p. 791).

2 "They call all the Sácae Scythians". (Herod: VII. 64.) The word really applies to a particular tribe, but is used loosely of all 'Scythians" by classical writers.

3 "The *general* mode is delineation in dogs and birds" (Justin 41. 3.)

4 Strabo. X. 5. 6.

5 " XI. 11. 8.

6 " XI. 8. 6. (Massa Pehlevi for "great"). Note especially what Strabo says of the Bactrian custom (XI. 1*h*, 3):—"The practice of the Caspii, with regard to their dead, is more tolerable than that of the Bactrians, *but the customs of the latter resemble the Scythian customs more closely*", unless we interpret the word σκυθικώτερον as merely meaning "more savage", in a general sense.

The fur-clad Anaitis[1], too, may have existed in Bactria at a period anterior to the coming of the Iranians. Her principal feast was called the "Sacea", and we may be tempted to think that the furs which were her chief ornament, like those of the god described by Cunningham[2], point to her being originally a Scythian or Sacæn deity from the cold north, where the Nomad tribes often wore seal-skin[3] and other furs. She was no doubt taken over and identified with the Iranian, and later the Hellenic, goddess by the process of 'Syncretism', which is a common phenomenon of later Greek religion.

The Iranian conquerors seem to have seized the hill fortresses, and to have established themselves there, as the Normans did in their castles in England: and hence we find the various strongholds to have been severally the abodes of the great Iranian lords, Oxyartes, Sismithres and others. These Iranians appear to have formed the 'knightly' or Equestrian class (for which again we go to Norman England, for a parallel), and the famous

---

1 *Anaitis*—See note on previous chapter. It may be here as well to draw attention to the significant fact that the Scythian invaders of Bactria were particularly devoted to her cult. Nano appears on nearly all their coins, particularly those of Kadphises. She is portrayed on a coin of Huviska.

2 Cunningham, Num: Chron: IX. 295.

3 *e.g.* The Massagetæ, Strabo XI, 8. 7.

Bactrian cavalry force was, perhaps, drawn solely from their numbers. This is the state of this we should, by analogy, expect, and its actual existence is strongly hinted at by some remarkable words of Curtius.

In describing one of the many outbreaks which rendered the reduction of Bactria and Sogdia such a colossal task to Alexander, Curtins says:—"Alexander was again checked by news of from revolt in Sogdia, which had spread over Bactria as well .... Spitamenes and Catenes had spread a rumour that Alexander was going to summon all the "Equites" and put them to death. *Now there were seven thousand of these whom the rest obeyed* (vii millia erant quorum auctoritati ceteri sequebantur ([1]))". These words seem to point to some sort of distinct standing accorded to the Equestrian body, and we can readily understand that this position would be confined strictly to the Iranian conquerors. Such a supposition, too, gives point to the story of the rumour. Alexander was going to complete the subjugation of Bactria by siding with the Helots in a massacre of their Iranian masters. Whether, as in Sparta, every Iranian bore arms is not known at all: the cavalry force numbered from seven to eleven thousand.

1 Curtius. VII. 6.

Evidently the Iranians were closely related to the Aryans of Northern India: between them, however, was a bitter rivalry. Perhaps the tillers of the rich Oxus valley suffered from plundering expeditions from beyond the Parapamisus; for, though the Brahmin and Zoroastrian creed have a common origin in the Vedic faith, the Indian Devas become the malignant spirits of the Zend-Avesta.

Tradition gives "Zoroaster" as the first king[1]. There is no real reason for suspecting the historical reality of great but shadowy character, though we have no more reliable information about him than about Lycurgus. "Perhaps", says Westcott[2], "Zarathushtra Spitama arose to organise his countrymen and purify their faith when the Aryan tribes of Bactria and North India were on the point of disruption". This would put the Iranian occupation of Bactria down to the middle of the 2nd millenium B.C. The hymns of the Zend-Avesta contain, as we have seen, one allusion at least, which seems to point to a Bactrian origin[3]. We

[1] Justin, 2. 3.

[2] Gospel of Life, s. v Zoroaster.

[3] *Literature of Bactria.*—Literature seems to be indebted to Bactria for the hymns of the Zend-Avesta.

It is curious to note that two common proverbs of the present day seem to have had a Bactrian origin. Cobares, speaking of Alexander to Bessus, said:—"His bark is worse than his bite; it is the still water which runs deep". (*Adjicit deinde quod apud Bactrianos vulgo usurpabant: canem timidum vehementius latrare quam mordere: altissima quoque flumina minimo sono labi*".)-Q. Crutius, VII. 4.

are also led to consider that Bactria was the cradle of the Zoroastrian creed by another fact: the purer or more extreme forms of the practices which Zarathushtra prescribed never seem to have spread further than Bactria, except among the Magi. The Persians buried their dead, first embalming them and covering them with a coat of wax to prevent contact with the sacred element, Earth[1]. Arrian, for instance, relates that Alexander sent the body of Darius to be interred in the royal mausoleum among the bodies of the king of his ancestors[2].

The stories which Justin and Diodorus (drawing, apparently, upon Ctesias for their information) relate concerning the history of Bactria during the Assyrian period, have, of course, no direct historic value. But they attest in a very interesting fashion to the immense antiquity of the advanced type of civilization in Bactria. Even in the remote age to which the legends apparently refer, the Bactrians or Bahlikas, as the Hindu accounts call them, were the rivals and foes of Nineveh itself. Bactria, according to classical story, was first conquered and added to Assyria by Ninus, who in his last war defeated and killed a Bactrian monarch, whom Diodorus calls

---

[1] Herodotus I. 140. (A sect of Parsis in Guzerat still *bury* their dead after bringing a *dog* to view the corpse).

[2] Anabasis. 3, 22, 1.

Oxyartes, but who is identified by Justin with Zoroaster himself. Legend further gives the Bactrians a prominent share in the attack which Arbaces made upon Nineveh in the days of Assurbanipal (Sardanapalus), resulting in the overthrow of the Assyrian Empire, and the fact is not without significance, as it indicates that Bactria had a military reputation at an early date; after this legend is silent for many years, and when Bactria again emerges upon the scene, we find ourselves upon surer ground.

Under the Persian Empire, Bactria was conquered by Cyrus, and the importance of the undertaking is emphasized by Herodotus, who informs us that Cyrus conducted the expedition in person, as a task too difficult to be left to a subordinate[1]. Cyrus recognized the real importance of Bactria to the vast and nebulous Persian Empire; he saw that its primary function was to act as a barrier, interposed to protect the Aryan civilization of Western Asia and Eastern Europe from the oncoming tide of Mongolian invasion. As Curtis says,[2] it was no doubt due to the proximity of the

1 *Satraps of Bactria.*—Of royal descent, we know of five :—Smerdis, son of Cyrus; Masistes and Hystaspes, brothers of Xerxes; Bessus, cousin of Darius Codomanus. We are in the dark about the gallant Dadarses of the Behistun Inscription.

2 See Note 25 below.

Scythians and the constant marauding raids to which their fertile lands were always liable, that the Bactrians owed those martial qualities, which made them at once such useful and such troublesome subjects to their Persian masters. Cyrus seems to have appreciated this, for he built the great city of Cyropolis, the last great outpost of the West, to keep watch and ward over the fords of the Jaxartes. It was he, too, who started the practice of placing a Prince of the Blood over Bactria as its Satrap; his son Smerdis, or Tanyoxarces, as Ctesias calls him, was the first governor of whom we hear. Bactria under the Persians occupied a position analogous to that of the Counties Palatine in Norman England, and its governors, like the Lords of the Marche, enjoyed privileges which compensated for the arduous nature of their task.

Darius Hystaspes, in his re-organization of the Empire, constituted Bactria as the twelfth Satrapy, and under him it paid into the Imperial Treasury the very respectable sum of 360 talents per annum. Under Darius we hear of a satrap of Bactria of the name of Dardases. Phraortes of Margiana had raised the standard of revolt, and it fell to the Lord of the Bactrian Marches to act as the Great King's viceregent. The Behistun Inscription tells us how

Darius sent word to his servant Dardases, governor of Bactria, and bade him, "Smite the people that own me not." This mission Dardases successfully accomplished. We may conjecture that, like the other Satraps of Bactria, Dardases was of royal descent, but we know nothing further of him.

In the reign of Xerxes, two of his brothers hold the Imperial Satrapy in turn. Prince Hystaspes, the elder of these, is chiefly known to us in connection with the great invasion of Greece in 480 B.C., when he appeared at the head of the Bactrian and Sacæan contingent. The troops who marched under Prince Hystaspes, however, appear to have been drawn from the lower orders, the helot or Sacæan portion of the population. They were scarcely to be distinguished, says Herodotus, from the other outlying contingents, whose equipment seems so futile, when we remember that they were destined to meet in the field the long pike and complete armour of the Greek Hoplite. Their uniform and arms consisted of "A Medic turban, bows of a kind of cane peculiar to Bactria, and short spears".[1] The cavalry were equipped in the same manner. These can hardly have been the same force as the famous Bactrian knights who

[1] Herodotus VII, 64.

won immortal renown in the operations against Alexander the Great. It may be that the Iranian horse did actually serve in this campaign, but that they were armed in the same way as the Persian heavy cavalry, and hence did not find a place in the picturesque catalogue of Book VII. It is noteworthy, however, that when Mardonius was selecting a picked force to carry on the campaign after the retreat of Xerxes, he chose "Medes, Sacae, Bactrians and Indians, both Infantry and Cavalry" (VIII 113), which attests to the military prowess of the Bactrian troops.

Hystaspes was apparently succeeded by Masistes, his brother, as governor of Bactria. Masistes had held a staff appointment under Mardonius during the Greek campaign; the tragic story of the court intrigue which led to his death, is one of the most vivid of the narratives with which Herodotus adorns his history. The wife of Xerxes, suspecting an intrigue between her husband and the wife of Masistes, forced the weak and guilty tyrant to put the woman into her power, and inflicted upon her the most horrible mutilations. Masistes left the court with his family, intending to raise his Satrapy in revolt and avenge the cruel insult in blood. Had he reached Bactria he would probably have caused great trouble as he had been a popular ruler; he was, however, intercepted and killed with all his family on the way.

Bactria appears to have been used as a sort of "Siberia" by the Persian Kings. The Persian commanders before the battle of Lade tried to coerce the wavering rebels with threats of "Transportation to Bactria."[1] It was also occasionally selected as a place for settling dispossessed subjects: Xerxes settled the Branchiadae here: after the Ionian revolt they had to flee from the wrath of their Greek neighbours as they were guilty of betraying the treasures of Apollo of Didymi to Persia.

We hear little more of Bactria till the days of Alexander.[2] The country was known to Greece, partly from its commercial importance (it was the great commercial *entrepôt* of the East) and partly from its connection with the legend of Bacchus. This legend was a link between East and West, and served as a convenient peg on which to hang many wondrous tales, for the "Mysterious East" was as

---

1 Herodotus VI. 9.—Rawlinson remarks that normally the *maidens* would have been sent to *Susa*, but Bactria would sound more terrible and distant, and add force to the threat. We never hear any more of the colony of Libyans from Barca, settled in Bactria by Darius. (Herodotus IV. 204).

2 For the history of Bactria under the Persian Empire, see Rawlinson's Herodotus, appendix to Book VII, which has been extensively used here.

fascinating to the ancient Greek as to the modern Englishman.[1]

At Gaugamela, a contingent[2] of Bactrian cavalry fought for Darius against the Greek invader with splendid but unavailing gallantry. The storming of the "Gates of Persia", convinced the advisers of Darius that their only chance of success now lay in falling back upon Ariana. The great provinces in the extreme East were as yet unaffected by the campaign which had wrested the West from the great king, and the followers of Zarathustra, who had been accustomed to practise their creed undisturbed for ages in the heart of their mountain-home, were likely to prepare a hot reception for the invader.[3] But the conduct of Darius had inspired little confidence in his followers. Bessus, prince of the province of Bactria, and cousin of the king, coveted the throne of a master who was now far less powerful than his kinsmen and subject, lord of a

---

[1] For instance, Euripides Bacchae. 1, 15.

[2] Only 1,000 strong. Why so small a force? Bersus may, even then, have been only lukewarm in his royalty.

[3] *Bactrian Courage.*—The courage of the Bactrians was proverbial. Curtius pays them a fine tribute of praise: "*Sunt autem Bactriani inter illas gentes promptissimi: horridis ingenis multumque a Persarum luxu abhorrentibus, siti haud procul Scytharum gente bellicosissima et rapto vivere assueta, semperque in armis erant.*" (IV. 6. 3.) (25).—See also what the author of the Periplus says, p. 27 (μαχιμώτατον ἔθνος......etc.)*

* It is significant that Curtius mentions that the luxury which had sapped the rest of Persia had not affected Bactria. Alexander's task really began when the campaign against Bassus was undertaken.

great and as yet intact province. And so when at last Alexander and his picked cavalry-men rode into the retreating rearguard at dawn, it was to find the last of the heirs of "Cyrus the king, the Achæmenian", lying amid his dead mules and drivers, stabbed through and through. Bessus was far ahead, gone to make a desperate effort to restore the fortunes of the Achæmenian dynasty in his own person at Bactria, with the title of Artaxerxes.

Alexander might have marched upon Bessus by the great northern trade route which ran (and still runs) from the Caspian through Hecatompylos and Antiochia Margiana (Merv) to Bactria.

The revolt of Satibarzanes, the satrap of Aria, however, could not be overlooked. It was a moral certainty that he would be joined by the other great provinces of the South, as they were ruled by a confederate of Bessus, Barsaentes. Alexander therefore suddenly changed his plans, and before anyone was aware of his approach, was under the walls of Herat (Artacoana, afterwards the Arian Alexandria). Satibarzanes had no alternative but to flee, and Alexander marching south, subdued the provinces of Drangiana (Seistan) and Gedrosia. It was the spring of 329, when the Macedonians began to march up the Helmand valley, and a year of climbing and fighting, found Alexander master of the Passes which led into Bactria *viâ* the Kabul defiles. Two strong cities put a seal on the new conquests, and secured the Greek rear,—a town which may be the modern Kandahar, and the Caucasian Alexandria, where seven thousand veterans were settled.[1] The Macedonians suffered severely from the hardships of the snowy and precipitous route they had followed. Hardly less trying was the heat and drought of the plains of Bactria, but the almost superhuman energy of Alexander and his marvellous men had the desired effect on the rebels.

No troops could be found to face the Greeks, and even the formidable Bactrian cavalry, who had once more rallied to the number of 8,000, to meet the invader, and might have inflicted severe losses on an exhausted army descending the mountain passes in more or less detached columns, their horses worn out and mostly dead, melted away, and Bessus was forced to evacuate the country. He crossed the Oxus and fell back on Nautaka in Sogdia, with only a small body of personal retainers, in the hope of rallying the Sacæ and Scythians from beyond the Jaxartes to his standard. Alexander meanwhile

[1] Q. C. VII. 3. Arrian. Anab: III. 28 and IV. 22.

was obliged to rest beneath the walls of Bactria. Trouble was brewing on all sides. Greece was restless, and Western Ariana ablaze with rebellion, the army was exhausted, and the cavalry unable to replace the horses which had been lost in the mountains[1]. Erygius, in charge of the troops there, was old, perhaps incapable of keeping open the lines of communication; before the weary Greeks lay the formidable deserts of Sogdiana, and the limitless plains of Scythia. Alexander solved the difficulty characteristically. He resolved on an immediate advance. Artabazus was left in charge of Bactria, and the army once more plunged into the desert. They marched by night to avoid the terrible midday sun: but in spite of all precautions, the suffering was terrible.

After great privations, the Oxus was reached. Alexander very characteristically refused to drink or unbuckle his armour till the last straggler came in: the army was close on the enemy's heels, in spite of the fact that Bessus had wasted the country in his flight, broken bridges, and destroyed the boats by which he had crossed the river.

---

1 Arrian Anab: III. 30. This was serious on account of the strength of the Bactrian Cavalry. Remounts could be got later on, horses being plentiful in the fertile parts of Bactria, but they were wanted on the spot.

The campaign was brought to an end by a quarrel between Bessus and his confederates, which ended by the surrender of the former to Ptolemy Lagus; a good deal of further fighting, however, was necessary before the country submitted to Alexander; and in one skirmish the king was wounded in the leg. Finally, however, some sort of order was restored; Maracanda, the capital of Sogdia, was taken, and the town of Alexandria Eschate was founded on the Jaxartes, to overawe the inhabitants, and to serve as an outpost against the Scythians beyond the river.

Mention must here be made of one trace of Greek civilization anterior to the coming of the Macedonians which Alexander found in this distant land. In the wild country on the confines of Bactria was the little colony of the Branchiadae. They had been settled in this remote village by Xerxes: they had originally come from Miletus, whence they had been forced to flee when the Greek cities of Asia finally threw off the Persian yoke. The little town, "the world forgetting, by the world forgot", was fast losing all traces of the language and customs of the land of its birth. The approach of the Greeks was enthusiastically welcomed: but Alexander, we are surprised to read, butchered the inhabitants and stamped the city out with the utmost ferocity. In extenuation, it is pleaded that Alexander was "visiting the sins of the fathers upon the children": that, in fact, he could do no less, as the leader of a great Pan-Hellenic army to avenge the invasion of Darius and Xerxes[1].

Alexander's troubles were by no means over; however, the Scythians, resenting the great fortress which they saw rising with incredible rapidity in their midst, were up in arms against the intruder; while further south, Spitamenes, the late confederate of Bessus, was blockading the Greek garrison in the Acropolis of Maracanda: and in Bactria an insurrection against Artabazus had been excited by a rumour, industriously circulated, that the flower of the Bactrian chivalry was to be seized and executed[2].

With the fall and destruction of the great city of Cyropolis and the capture of Gaza[3], the rebellion was considerably checked, and an advance in force against the Scythians was begun. This terminated successfully; the Scythians came to terms and Alexander once more turned his attention to Bactria. Spitamenes was forced to flee, and Maracanda

1 Strabo XI. 11. 4. Curtius VII 5. Not a word of this appears in Arrian. Were his authorities too ashamed of the "deed of blood" to record it?

2 Curtius VII. 6.—*vide* Arrian IV. 1. *sub fin.*

3 Arrian IV. 2. Curtius (VII. 6) says "another city."

became the centre of operations. One city, a rocky and almost inaccessible fortress, still held out. "Can you fly?" said Arimazes scornfully, in reply to a summons to surrender. Alexander proved that flying was not necessary: and when a picked body of three hundred, after incredible exertions, had seized a point of vantage, the rock-fortress opened its gates. Arimazes was crucified, as a warning to offenders in the future, and by a policy partly of severity, partly of conciliation, Sogdiana and Bactria were pacified. A chain of forts, "velut freni domitarum gentium" says Curtius, was established near Margiana, to protect, perhaps, the western frontier, as Alexandria Eschate protected the eastern[1]. Peucolaus managed to govern Sogdiana with a standing force of only 3,000 infantry: this is a striking testimony to the completeness of Alexander's subjugation.

Artabazus was relieved of his command, on the plea of advancing years, and the province of Bactria was handed over to Clitus. It was while the army was wintering at Maracanda, on the eve of his departure to take over this important command, that the unfortunate brawl took place, in which he lost

---

[1] Curtius VII. 10. fin. Curtius says "*Superatis Oxo et Ocho ad urbem Marginiam pervenit*". The forts were to keep back the Dahae, who only surrendered after the news of the death of Spitamenes.

his life[1]. His place was taken by Amyntas[2]. Trouble once more seemed imminent, when, during Alexander's absence on a final visit to Sogdia, Spitamenes once more appeared in Bactria, with a motley force of Scythian malcontents and Sogdian exiles, and a considerable body of cavalry, raised from the Massagetae. Spitamenes appears to have been a general of some ability; he again succeeded in inflicting considerable losses on the Macedonian army of occupation, and ambushed a punitive expedition sent against him with complete success. On the approach of the royal army, however, he was overtaken by the fate which, through his instrumentality, had befallen his former confederate; he was betrayed by his own party[3]; and his head was brought to the king as a peace-offering.

It was now winter[4], and the Macedonian forces were ordered into quarters, to await the arrival of the recruits which were being raised all over Asia Minor. The army had suffered considerably in the operations of the previous autumn, it was further depleted by the necessity of leaving a considerable

---

1 Arrian seems to think that this took place at Zariaspa, but it is more probable that it was at Maracanda, his head-quarters in the north.

2 Curtius VIII. I. -Arrian IV. 17. The latter does not mention Clitus, but there is no reason why we should doubt Curtius.

3 So Arrian, Anab: IV, 17. *fin.* Curtius makes his wife murder him.

4 338-7 B. C.

force in occupation and by the numerous colonies of veterans which had been founded.

Early next spring Alexander moved out to reduce more of those rock-fortresses, so characteristic of the country; it was impossible to leave for India while they still resisted. The great Sogdian rock, the key of eastern Sogdiana, was strongly held by the Iranian Oxyartes, but was surrendered when a party of Alexander's wonderful troops scaled the rock by night and were found in the morning in a position overlooking the defences. About this time Alexander took the very characteristic step of marrying the beautiful Iranian Roxane. Who this Roxane was is not quite clear. Arrian, Strabo and Diodorus Siculus[2] concur in describing her as the daughter of Oxyartes, who, with her mother, fell into Alexander's hands on the fall of the Sogdian rock. Curtius however calls her the daughter of one "Cohortanus", a person of whom we never again hear, unless he meant Chorienes[3]. According to the account in Curtius, the maiden was brought in with thirty other Sogdian virgins after a banquet given to the victorious king and his staff, for a

---

1 Roxana, *i.e.*, Rosn-ak "Little Star". See appendix to the chapter.

2 Strabo XI. II. 4. Diodorus. XVIII, 3. 5.

3 Arrian Anab. IV. 21. Q. Curtius, VIII, 4, 23. (16).

less noble purpose. But Alexander, struck by her modest beauty, solemnly espoused after the simple Macedonian rite, offering her bread divided with the sword, of which each partook. Whichever story be true, and the details are historically unimportant. Alexander acted partly with that fine chivalry which never quite deserted him, and partly from motives of policy. He was leaving for India, and wished to have a settled country in his rear. Curtius would have us believe that this marriage offended the proud Macedonian nobility. However, Seleucus, one of the proudest, followed suit by marrying Apama, daughter of the dead Spitamenes, and the soldiery were freely encouraged by example and reward to take Iranian wives and settle in accordance with Alexander's scheme for hellenizing and permanently securing his conquests. Garrison towns had sprung up in all directions; the number of Greco-Macedonian settlers, including the army of occupation, was probably considerably over 20,000[1]. They were not however of the highest character. Justin expressly says that Alexander took the opportunity

---

[1] *Strength of the Greek forces in Bactria.*

The Army under Amyntas was 11,500 (Arrian Anab: IV. 22). We know that 23,000 went home on Alexander's death and 7,000 had been settled in the Caucasian Alexandria. Considerable garrisons were in the forts near Margiana, in Maracanda, Bactria, and other towns. Alexander founded twelve cities in Bactria alone. Alexandria Eschate was largely populated with natives from the city of Cyropolis, when the latter was destroyed.

to get rid of the men he could not trust in a campaign which, he foresaw, must be trying to the most loyal of troops. "He built twelve towns in Sogdiana and Bactria, and he distributed among them the men he found inclined to be mutinous."[1] Alexander was no sooner out of the way, than these turbulent spirits caused considerable trouble[2]. They mutinied, and then, fearing the consequences, broke into open revolt, much to the consternation of the populace, who suffered considerably. Finally, they seized the citadels of Bactria and proclaimed one of their number Athenodorus king. Their idea seems to have been rather to evacuate the country and disperse homewards than actually to set up an independent kingdom; whatever their intention, however, it was cut short by the murder of their leader. Further conspiracies followed, till at last the soldiery, sick of plots and counter-plots, released Bico, one of those implicated, and under his leadership left Bactria for ever[3]. Amyntas no doubt found his task considerably simplified by their departure.

Bactria appears to have enjoyed some internal peace after these events. The inhabitants of the mountainous districts of Parapamisus, however,

---

1 Justin. XI. 6. *fin.*
2 Curtius IX. 7.
3 Curtius *may* be relating what really happened *after* Alexander's death. The story lacks confirmation.

appear to have suffered considerably from the extortionate and high-handed conduct of their governor Tyriaspes[1], and complaints of his conduct reached Alexander when the latter was encamped at the confluence of the Acesines and the Indus. He was executed, and his satrapy was handed over to Oxyartes[2], the father of Roxane. Oxyartes appears to have been given some subordinate command after his surrender; he was suspected of complicity in the late troubles of Bactria, but pleaded his cause in person before the king,—with complete success, as appears from the words of Curtius. He continued to hold his command after Alexander's death. That great catastrophe fell like a thunnderbolt on the far eastern dependencies of the Macedonian empire. No one knew what would be the next move; the mighty kingdom was like a rudderless ship; and 23,000 soldiers left Bactria in wild panic, marching on Babylon they demanded repatriation[3].

Authorities differ considerably as to who obtained Bactria in the division of the empire. Justin

---

1 *Tyriaspes.* He is called Tirystes by Arrian VI. 15 and Terioltes by Curtius IX. 8.

2 I have identified him with Oxathres. Curtius says: "*Oxathres prætor Bactrianorum non absolutus modo sed etiam jure amplioris imperii donatus est.*" Diodorus calls him a "Bactrian King". Both are vague expressions; probably they only signify that Oxyartes was *a* ruler (not *the* ruler) in *a part* of Bactria *ulterior*).

3 Pithon, Satrap of Media, appears to have exterminated them. Diodorus Siculus XVIII 7.

and the late historian Orosius[1] assert that Amyntas remained in charge of Bactria. They assign Sogdia, however, to one Scythaeus, of whom nothing more is known. This is contradicted by Diodorus and Dexippus[2], who seem to concur in giving Bactria and Sogdia to "Philip the praetor". Photius[3] says that Arrian (in his lost work on the Division of the Empire) assigned Sogdia and Bactria to Stasanor of Soli. The question however is not one of great importance. Probably two divisions of the empire are inextricably confused. Amyntas may have died[4] shortly after Alexander, after which Philip, who appears to have been in charge of Parthia, was given the whole or part of Bactria; possibly he had been assigned Sogdia previously, and afterwards took charge of Bactria as well.

On the death of Perdiccas, a redistribution of offices took place throughout the empire. This second partition, known as the partition of Triparadisus, took place in 321 B. C., and it was then that Stasanor of Soli was allotted Bactria and Sogdia, Stasander the Cypriot being at the same time appointed

---

1 The Spanish Chronicler, Circa 400 A. D. His Universal History was immensely popular in the Middle Ages.

2 Apud Photium, Bibliothec: LXXXI.

3 Do. XCII.

4 Or, as Bevan thinks, was dismissed for incompetence (after the revolt of the mercenaries). Perhaps the experiment of putting a native in a position of authority was not a success.

to the neighbouring provinces of Drangiana and Aria[1]. We know that Stasanor was still in charge in 316 B. C., for Diodorus records the fact that Antigonus dared not replace him[2]. Oxyartes continued in office as Satrap of the Kabul valley, and possibly both he and Stasanor assumed a semi-independent position soon after the death of Alexander. Hence, perhaps, Diodorus is led to call him a "Bactrian king". Or is Diodorus thinking of Plutarch's assertion that Oxyartes was a brother of Darius? The Satrapy of the Kabul or Parapamisus extended to the Cophenes or Kabul river, and as controlling the Khyber Pass, was, as Alexander perceived, of considerable importance. It is probable that Oxyartes continued to hold his position till Chandragupta (303 B. C.) brought Seleucus Nicator to his knees, and forced the "ever-victorious" monarch to cede the Province of Kabul, together, probably with Arachosia, Aria, and at any rate, a part of Gedrosia. The other Greek rulers in India[3] (Pithon Eudamus and the rest) had been swept away long before.

---

1 Diodorus Siculus. XVIII. 9. Mc.Crindle mixes them up "Invasion of India", p 411. V. A. Smith ignores Philip (Early History of India, p 109).

2 XIX. 48.

3 A colleague of Oxyartes. Arrian Anab: VI. 15. But the text must be corrupt; Pithon was in charge of the Lower Indus.

APPENDIX TO CHAPTER II.

The Story of Roxana.—With the strange eventful history of this unhappy girl, we have not now to deal. It is worth while, however, noticing the reference to the story of her wedding in the "Sikander Nama", the mediæval Persian poem (or series of poems) on the adventures (more or less mythical) of Alexander in Persia and India. These legends grew round the name of the greatest personality that ever impressed itself upon the East, just as mediæval legends grew round the magic name of Virgil. In Canto XXXIII of the Sikander Nama, Sikander weds Roshan or Roshan-ak (Roxana) *Dara's daughter.* (Roshan means a 'torch' or 'light' (perhaps a 'star') and *ak* is an 'affectionate' diminutive.) The remarkable thing about the passage is, that Roxana is made out to be the daughter of *Darius.* This is very interesting, for it confirms Plutarch's assertion to a certain extent, that Oxyartes was a *brother of Darius.* I add Plutarch's account of the marriage, for purposes of comparison. It forms an interesting corollary to the accounts of other authors. "Alexander's marriage with Roxana, the daughter of Oxyartes, brother of Darius, a chieftain of Sogdiana (with the exception of the wife of Darius, the loveliest woman seen by the Macedonians) was entirely the effect of love. He saw her at an entertainment, and found her charms irresistible. Nor was the match unsuitable to the political situation. The barbarians placed great confidence in him on account of that alliance, and his chastity gained their affection. It delighted them to think he would not approach the only woman he passionately loved, without the sanction of marriage". (Langhorne's Translation p. 478). For the "Sikander Nama" see Captain H. Wilberforce Clark's Translation. The subject may be further pursued in Professor Rehatseks', article "The Alexander Myth" in the J. B. B. R. A. S. XV. p. 37—64 (Jan. 24th 1881).

Dara 'Lord', is a title rather than a name, cf "Arsaces".

CHAPTER III.

THE ESTABLISHMENT OF BACTRIAN INDEPENDENCE.

ON the death of Alexander, the huge edifice, which the master-mind had built up, melted away almost as quickly as it had sprung up into being. Alexander had done all that forethought and policy could suggest to consolidate his conquests on his march to the East but he was removed before the schemes he had set in motion had time to mature. His officers had learned only too well the lessons which Alexander the General had to teach: Alexander the apostle of Hellenism, the founder of a cosmopolitan world-empire, they utterly failed to comprehend.

At first Perdiccas, by virtue of his personal ascendency, established a temporary *modus vivendi*, with himself as regent; he lacked, however, the magic personality of his great predecessor, and in a short time the mutual rivalry of the generals plunged Asia into war, Perdiccas himself finding his death on the banks of the Nile at the hands of his own troopers.

One of the most distressing of the effects of Alexander's untimely end was that the Macedonian invasion of the East, instead of consolidating the various Asiatic nations into a great Hellenic State, in which the immense resources of the Persian empire were turned to proper account, resulted merely in bitter discord and further disintegration. The Macedonian troops, who had marched across half a continent to accomplish what had been perhaps the greatest project which human enterprise has ever conceived, were now, as a reward for their labours, set at one another's throats, and the mild, if ineffective, government of the Achemaenides was exchanged for something infinitely worse—the tyranny of a foreign military autocracy, who turned the country which they had conquered into a battle-field of rival factions.

After the death of Perdiccas, a second and somewhat more successful attempt at a settlement was made in 321 B.C. at the conference of Triparadisus. From this time two great personalities emerge from the confused tangle of contending forces—Seleucus and Antigonus. Seleucus, now satrap of Babylon, was obliged by motives of policy to side with his rival in the struggle against Eumenes, but Antigonus saw in a confederate so indispensable a more than probable rival, and Seleucus only anticipated the fate of Eumenes and Pithon by a providential escape into Egypt with a handful of horse. In 312 B.C., however, we find him back in Babylon, casting about for means to establish an empire whose resources would enable him to meet his great rival in the West. Whither could he better turn than to the East? The clash of arms which reverberated through these unquiet years from end to end of Asia Minor only awoke distant echoes in the far eastern frontier. East of the Cophenes, Macedonian influence was steadily on the decline, the generals who had conquered the East being far too busy with the task of destroying one another to keep an eye on the government of the lands which had cost them so much blood and labour to acquire. Pithon, the ruler of Scind, had been compelled to vacate his command by 320 B.C. Eudamus, in command of the garrison at Alexandria-on-Indus, went home (after murdering his native colleague and collecting all the plunder he could lay hands on,[1]) with a body of troops, to participate in the scramble for power, in 317 B. C., probably only anticipating expulsion by voluntary evacuation.

West of the Cophenes, Stasanor continued to govern Bactria, and Oxyartes the province which

[1] Diodorus XIX, 4.

lies in the triangle between the Indus and Cophenes and the Parapamisus range.

The kinsman of Darius even appears to have sent help to the confederates in the war with Antigonus, but was allowed to remain unmolested. Perhaps, on the receipt of the news of the tragic end of his daughter and grandson, he changed sides, or withdrew from the contest; his influence, in any case, was of no weight on either side. In 306 B. C. the peace of Bactria was once more disturbed. Seleucus entered the country and demanded their allegiance. We may imagine that it was given without any prolonged resistance, as Justin passes over the fact in a single sentence [1]. But when once more the glint of Macedonian pikes was descried on the winding road descending the Kabul Pass, India was ready to meet her invaders on more equal terms. Chandragupta [2], the first of the Mauryas, had seized the throne of Magadha, expelling the last of the Nandas, whose weak and unpopular rule had made India an easy prey to all comers.

Chandragupta had studied in the school of Alexander, and had learnt much from the great general whom he worshipped as a hero of semi-

1 "*Principio Babylona cepit; inde, auctis ex victoria viribus, Bactrianos expugnavit*". Justin XV. 4. This is condensation with a vengeance.

2 Sandracottus.

divine powers. What happened in the encounter we do not know. Probably Seleucus recognized the futility of a struggle when he found his opponents in such unexpected strength [1], particularly in view of his coming in conflict with Antigonus. Terms were concluded satisfactorily to both, and while Seleucus returned with his forces considerably augmented by Indian elephants and, no doubt, subsidies from Bactria, Chandragupta was allowed to extend his domains up to the edge of the Parapamisus, probably including in his territory Arachosia and part of Gedrosia. They were useless to a ruler engaged in a life and death struggle two thousand miles away: and, unlike Bactria, were not valuable as supplying subsidies of men or money to any extent.

At Ipsus (301 B. C.) Antigonus fell, and Asia passed into the hands of Seleucus. For fifty years we hear nothing of Bactria. The 'rowdy' element, it will be remembered, had passed out of the land on the death of Alexander, to find their fate at the swords of Pithon's troops. The remaining Greeks

---

1 600,000 infantry, 30,000 cavalry and 9,000 elephants. V. A Smith "Early History of India", p. 117 (2nd Edition). But it is unwarranted to talk of Seleucus as 'defeated' or 'humbled', as Smith does. Our authorities imply nothing of the kind. It was a compromise; Seleucus gave up lands over which he had never been able to exercise a *de facto* sovereignty, in return for a lucrative alliance. The actual terms are disputed. For the *pros* and *cons* see Smith, Appendix G (p. 152) of his "History of India."

appear to have intermarried with the Iranian populace, and to have settled down peacefully under the rule of the Greek satrap: even in religion, a compromise appears to have been effected, the Greeks recognizing in Anahid of Bactria their own Artemis or Venus. In 281 B. C., Seleucus fell by the blow of an assassin, and in the endless and insensate struggle which ensued between Syria and Egypt, Bactria seized an obvious opportunity to cast off a yoke which had become little more than nominal. Antiochus II (Theos) succeeded his father (of the same name) in 260 B. C. He carried on the futile campaigns against his neighbours, and it was not long ere the inhabitants of Parthia and Bactria recognized the folly of paying tribute to a distant monarch who was incapable of enforcing respect or obedience.

The details of this great revolt, which wrested from Syria the fairest jewel of her crown, and established one of the most remarkable of the many offshoots of Hellenic Colonial enterprise in the heart of Asia, are somewhat obscure. Bactria had enormously increased in power with fifty years' almost continuous peace; and Justin's mention of the "thousand cities" ruled over by the prefect of Bactria conveys a general notion of the prosperity of the country. The prefect of Bactria had furthermore, it seems, acquired a certain overlordship over the satrap of the country which afterwards became famous as Parthia [1]. This small tract of land, comprising chiefly the Tejend watershed, was quite insignificant when compared with the vast tracts of Bactria and Sogdiana, but contained a breed of men antagonistic from every point of view to the province which claimed their homage—they were non-Aryan, accustomed to plunder their more civilized neighbours, and born fighting men. Their satrap at the time appears to have been one Andragoras, who may have succeeded on the death of Stasanor. We cannot, perhaps, do better than to consider what Justin (our chief authority) has to say about the revolt.

"After the death of Antigonus", says Justin,[2] "the Parthians were under the rule of Seleucus Nicator, and then under Antiochus and his successors, from whose great-grandson, Seleucus, they revolted, at the time of the first Punic war, in the Consulship of Lucius Manilius Vulso and Marcus Attilius Regulus. For their revolt, the disputes

---

1 I infer this from what Strabo says of Arsaces :—"According to one account, he was a *Bactrian*, who withdrew himself from the encroachments of Diodotus, and established Parthia as an independent State". XI, 9, 3.

2 Justin XLI. 4-5.

between the brothers Antigonus and Seleucus gave them impunity; for the two latter were so intent on ousting one another from the throne that they neglected to chastise the revolters. *At the same period also,* Theodotus, governor of one thousand cities in Bactria, rebelled, and took the kingly title whereupon the other nations of the east, following his lead, fell away from Macedon, too. One Arsaces, a man of uncertain origin but undoubted courage, arose at this period. He was accustomed to make his livelihood as a bandit, and heard a report that Seleucus had been worsted by the Gauls in Asia. Feeling himself safe from interference, Arsaces invaded Parthia with a band of brigands, defeated and killed Andragoras, the governor, and took the reins of Government into his own hands".

This is by far the fullest account of the revolution which we possess, and it is more than usually full of Justin's usual inaccuracies. First of all what does Justin consider the date of the revolt to have been? He mentions "the Consulship of L. Manilius Vulso and M. Attilius Regulus". This was the year 256 B. C. Supposing however that M. Attilius is a mistake for C. Attilius, who was Consul with L. Manilius Vulso in 250 B. C., the latter date would be that of the revolt[1] and this agrees with the opinion of later authorities,[2] who place the revolt in "the eleventh year of Antiochus II". What Justin means by going on to refer to the "fraternal war" between Seleucus and Antiochus, or to the "report of a reverse suffered at the hands of the Gauls," I am unable to determine. The "fraternal war" broke out on the death of Antiochus Theus in 246, between Seleucus Callinicus and Antiochus Hierax, but if this is the case, why mention the consuls for the year 250 B. C.?

Perhaps Justin is confusing two separate accounts, and we may reconstruct the story of the revolt as follows :—

In 250 B. C. Diodotus revolted (while Antiochus Theus was busy with his Egyptian war) and Andragoras as his vassal followed suit. The revolutions were practically simultaneous,[3] but Bactria set the example. But the native Parthians cordially hated their rivals and masters on racial and other grounds, and in the years between 246 B.C. and 240 B. C. (the reference to the "reverse at the hands of the Gauls" must refer to rumours about the battle of Ancyra in 240 B. C.), a patriotic Parthian, who had

---

1 I follow, with some reservations, Rawlinson's "Sixth Oriental Monarchy", p. 44, note

2 Eusebius (Chronicle II. p. 32.). Moses of Chorene (History [Armenia, II. 1. fin).

3 "*Fodem tempore*, Theodotus——" Justin XLI. 4

taken upon himself the royal title of Arsaces[1], returned from exile among the Parnian Dahæ, of the same race as himself[2] in the Ochus valley, whence he had been carrying on a border war since his banishment and slew Andragoras[3]. He then proceeded to set up a purely native state, strongly anti-Hellenic, in which all traces of Alexander's influence were effaced. This, however, is at best a conjectural version of the story and takes no account of the assertion of Arrian[4], that the revolt was against Pherecles, Satrap of Antiochus Theus.

It seems fairly clear, however, that Diodotus revolted in the reign of Antiochus Theus, and this theory finds some support in the coins of Bactria which have been handed down to us. In Professor Gardner's "Coins of the Seleucid Kings of Syria"[5], we find figured one series which bears the inscription of Antiochus II, but a portrait which is certainly that of Diodotus, as figured in his coins. Did Diodotus, as Professer Gardner thinks, issue these coins, as a first tentative step towards open rebellion, "to supplant his master in the eyes of the

---

1 Arsa-kes (of the Scythian Maua-kes) was a title, not a name as Justin remarks, XLI. 5.

2 Strabo, IX, 9. 2.

3 Justin XLI. 5.

4 Fragment I.

5 Plate V., 7.

people"? It may well be so, and we may conjecture that he did not venture into open revolt until he found this first advance unreproved by the Syrian monarch[1].

Other authorities, relying on the fact that the face of the coins is that of a young man, consider the whole series to belong to the younger Diodotus, and that the father issued no coins in his own name at all[2]. In support of this theory, it must be remembered that Diodotus I. appears to have died in 245 B. C. (if we date the change in policy towards Parthia from his death), and coins would scarcely have the same opportunity of passing into general circulation as they would in the long reign of his son[3]. The Bactrian coins are all particularly fine and interesting, and those of the Diodoti are among the best. The cognizance of the Diodoti, before and after the revolt, appears to have been the figure of "Zeus thundering". Von Sallet puts down to Bactria, before the revolt, the silver coins[4] bearing

1 For discussion of the whole question of dates in connection with the two revolts, see Rawlinson. Sixth Oriental Monarchy, Chap. III; Beven's House of Seleucus, I, page 286, and V. A Smith, History of India, P. 196.

2 V. A. Smith, 'Catalague of. Coins in Calcutta Museum' Introduction and notes, pages 6 and 7.

3 In dealing with Euthydemus, we shall observe that he claims "to have destroyed the *Children of those who first rebelled*". This surely implies that Strabo believed in the existence of *two* rulers of the name of Diodotus, the *second* of the two being the one whom Euthydemus murdered.

4 I. M. 7616 and 9304.

the bust of Antiochus II. on the reverse and on the obverse, Zeus, striding to the left and hurling a bolt. These may belong to the period of Diodotus I. and the coins mentioned above as bearing the types and names of Antiochus, and the portrait of Diodotus may have been the earliest issue of his son.

Other fine coins of Diodotus (father or son—the face is always the same, and is that of a young man, clean shaven, with a severe but purely Hellenic type of features,)—are the gold one pictured by Professor Rapson[1], and the silver ones figured by Gardner in his catalogue[2]. All bear the image of the "Thundering Zeus," striding to the left and hurling his bolt on the reverse. One bronze coin only bears a figure of Artemis with torch and hound, and on the obverse a head which may be that of Zeus[3].

It has been already remarked that there was no love lost between the Bactrians and their fellow revolters—the Parthians. The Parthians, who immediately followed the lead of their powerful neighbours, did not win complete freedom for some years afterwards, probably, as we have seen, not till after the accession of Seleucus Callinicus; and apparently

1 In his article on Greek and Scythian coins contributed to the "Gundriss der Indo-Arischen Philologie".

2 Gardner "Catalogue of Greek and Scythic Kings" &c. Plate I. Nos. 4 to 8.

3 Ditto Plate I, 9.

Arsaces dreaded Bactria a good deal more than Syria.

The year 247 B. C. witnessed the meteoric invasion of Syria by Ptolemy Euergetes, who penetrated to the very borders of Bactria, without, however, entering the newly constructed kingdom, as far as we can judge. The expedition stopped short at this point, owing to domestic sedition, and the invasion of Ptolemy was only one more incident of the cruel and useless war that was draining the life-blood of Western Asia. Tiridates (or Arsaces II, for his brother, the great founder of Parthia, had fallen in battle,) now proceeded to annex Hyrcania, and shortly after took the surprising step of coming to terms with Bactria.

This effectually disposes of the theory that Diodotus II only existed in the pages of Trogus and Justin[1]: the alliance could never have been made in the reign of the first Diodotus, the determined opponent of Parthia, and the strongest foe to Arsaces, even from motives of fear; for it is not likely that the "prefect of a thousand cities" would fear a discredited and harassed monarch like Seleucus.

It is more likely that the treaty was concluded, as Justin says, by the second Diodotus, and that,

---

1 Introduction to Gardner's Catalogue.

just before the advance of Seleucus to subdue the invader of Hyrcania, whose challenge could hardly be overlooked. We may conclude, then, that Diodotus II succeeded his father, some time between the acquisition of Hyrcania by Parthia, and the invasion of Seleucus. Common consent has fixed the date at about 245 B. C.; Diodotus reigned till 230 B. C., and probably lived to regret the unnatural alliance he formed in his early youth, for Tiridates, thanks to his complaisance, won a complete and unexpected victory over the "ever-victorious" Seleucid, and launched Parthia on its great career, as the rival, not only of Bactria or Syria but Rome itself.[1]

Diodotus fell the victim of a court conspiracy, at the hands of one Euthydemus, a Magnesian, who appears to have taken effectual means to prevent any of the rival family from disputing his right to the throne. Is it possible that the murder was caused by discontent at the tame policy of Diodotus, who appears to have done little for Bactria in comparison with his successors, and certainly committed a fatal error of policy in his alliance with Parthia. Diodotus appears to have fallen some years before Antiochus III appeared on the throne of Syria, which was as well for the sake of Bactrian

1 Date uncertain Rawlinson, Sixth Oriental Monarchy, page 48, says 337 B. C. But is this not too late ?

freedom. His death probably took place about 230 B. C., after which a great change takes place in Bactrian policy, marked by a corresponding cessation of activity by the Parthians.

So ended the dynasty which founded Bactria as a free State ; in themselves not remarkable, later monarchs[1] were glad to claim kinship with the earliest kings of Bactria, and even to give Diodotus I the title of " Divine ".

---

1 Agathocles. See his coins in Gardner. (Plate IV. and Introduction pages XXVIIJ-XXIX)

APPENDIX TO CHAPTER III.

Antimachus "Theos".—This mysterious king, whose title would lead us to suppose him to be a personage of some importance, is only known to us from coins; historians have overlooked him. He appears to have been a son or close relation of Diodotus II, as his coins bear on the obverse that king's head, and on the reverse the naked Zeus hurling the bolt. V. A. Smith (p. 10 Catalogue of Coins in Calcutta Museum,) thinks "he succeeded Diodotus II in Kabul." But surely Kabul was at this time in the hands of Chandragupta[1]?

He appears to have been a member of the royal house, who, on the murder of Diodotus II proclaimed himself as the rightful heir, the inscription on the coins—ΒΑΣΙΛΕΥΟΝΤΟΣ ΑΝΤΙΜΑΧΟΥ ΘΕΟΥ—is that of a man who wished to emphasize his "divine right" to the throne, and after a brief reign as the head of "the legitimist faction", was quietly crushed by Euthydemus.

---

[1] See however V. A. Smith: Early History of India, p. 194.

CHAPTER IV.

BACTRIA AT THE HEIGHT OF ITS POWER.

IT must have been about the year 230 B. C. that Euthydemus, the Magnesian, murdered Diodotus and usurped his throne. Who Euthydemus was is quite unknown; but no doubt a Kingdom with the romantic history of Bactria appealed to the Greek imagination and attracted many "soldiers of fortune" ready to make a bid for success in the new world which had just been thrown open to them.

The treachery of Euthydemus was palliated, if not justified, by its success; under him and his successors Bactria not only magnificiently vindicated her rights to an independent existence, but launched upon a career of conquest and expansion which paralysed her rivals, and was destined to spread Hellenic influence more surely and permanently than had been done by the great Macedonian himself. So remarkable is the career of Euthydemus, that later historians forget the existence of Diodotus: "The house of Euthydemus", says Strabo, "was the first to establish Bactrian independence."[1] It is

[1] He is thinking of the successful repulse of Antiochus: before this, Bactria was only a kingdom "on sufferance."

possible, indeed, that the weak and vacillating policy of Diodotus particularly towards Bactria's national and well-hated rival, Parthia, was to a large degree responsible for his murder, which could hardly have taken place without the connivance of at least the great Iranian nobles.

Euthydemus had some years of uneventful prosperity, in which to consolidate the Empire he had seized, before he was challenged to vindicate his right by the ordeal of war. In 223 B.C. Antiochus III, second son of Seleucus Callinicus, succeeded to the throne of Syria. Antiochus has some right to the title of "The Great", which he assumed; he is one of the few Syrian monarchs for whom we can feel any real respect, combining as he did the personal valour which had become a tradition among the successors of Alexander's generals, with a military talent and a reluctance to waste the resources of his kingdom in interminable petty campaigns, which is only too rare in his predecessors.

It was only in reply to a direct challenge from Parthia, that Antiochus interfered at all in what was taking place in the East of his dominions. Artabanus I, (who succeeded Tiridates I. about 214 B. C.) pursuing the policy of aggression which under his predecessors had succeeded so admirably, took advantage of the rebellion of a satrap named Achaeus, to advance and occupy Media. This was open defiance, and Antiochus could not ignore it if he would. An arduous campaign followed; Antiochus did not make the mistake of underrating his foe, and Justin even puts his forces at 100,000 infantry and 20,000 cavalry.[1] However, the Parthians merely fell back further and further into their mountain fastnesses, and at length the dogged courage of Artabanus found its own reward.

The independence for which Parthia had fought so well and so persistently was at last recognized, and Antiochus even condescended to form an alliance with his gallant antagonist,[2] though lesser Media was restored to Syria. Perhaps, however, it was Artabanus who suggested to Antiochus the invasion of the rival state of Bactria, and he may even have lent him troops or promised co-operation. He may have pointed out to Antiochus what was fast becoming apparent, that Bactria, under the peaceful rule of Euthydemus, with its great natural resources, and the advantage of an enterprising Greek to direct its fortunes, was fast becoming a menace to Parthia and Syria alike. Besides, it would be a triumph of diplomacy, if Parthia could divert the forces of so

[1] Justin, XVI, 5.
[2] *Ibid*: "Postremum in societatem ejus admissus."

dreaded a neighbour against her cherished rival. Whichever way the fortunes of war might veer, Parthia must be the gainer. If Antiochus were successful, the fidelity and assistance of Artabanus might be rewarded by the control of Bactria, and at the least, Bactrian aggression would be checked for ever; on the other hand, if the Syrian forces were defeated, anarchy would no doubt soon reign once more in Syria, and Parthia would find her opportunity for further expansion once again. Antiochus had an excuse at hand for yielding to the arguments of Artabanus, if indeed we are right in supposing the Syrian monarch to have been influenced in his action by his new ally. Bactria had incurred the enmity of the Seleucids in the reign of the last monarch; the weak and short-sighted policy of Diodotus II. had enabled Parthia to establish her independence, as we have seen, unmolested; and above all, the Syrian Empire, rich though it was, almost exhausted, by years of sucidal war and misgovernment, and could ill afford the loss of the most fertile of her provinces, "the glory of Iran",[1] as it was popularly called. To regain the allegiance of of Bactria was a natural ambition.

The expedition against Bactria must have started in the year 209 B. C., perhaps in the early spring.

[1] Strabo Geog. XI, 11, 1.

Antiochus chose to attack the country by approaching from the south and striking at the capital.

The campaign has been described by Polybius[1] in the concise vivid style which gives the reader so ready an impression of military operations: unfortunately the chapter is an isolated fragment only, and breaks off after a description of the battle with which the campaign opened, leaving all account of the subsequent operations a blank. Of the invasion, however, the ravages of time have spared us a minute account. Antiochus marched along the Southern borders of the Arius,[2] the river which rises in the Hindu-Kush, and loses itself, like so many rivers in that region, in the shifting sands and fertile patches just beyond the Tejend Oasis. The invader had of necessity to choose his route in a march upon Bactria, if he was to avoid the hardships and perils of the Bactrian wastes.

He learnt that the ford[3] by which he intended to cross into the enemy's territory was held in force by the famous Bactrian cavalry; and to attempt to force a passage in the face of these, was to court disaster. Knowing, however, that it was a Bactrian custom

---

1 Polybius. XI, 34 & X, 49.
2 The Hari-Rud.
3 Close to a city called by Polybius Ταγουρίαν: Von Gutschmid emends to Τὰ Γαυρίανα. The ford was a little to the west of the town.

to withdraw their main force, leaving a thin screen of pickets to hold the positions occupied, Antiochus determined on a bold bid for success. Leaving his main Army behind, he advanced swiftly and suddenly with a picked body of Cavalry and attacked, probably at dawn, so unexpectedly that he carried the passage almost unopposed, driving the pickets back upon the main body. A fierce encounter now took between the picked horsemen of Iran and Syria. Antiochus, with the recklessness characteristic of the successors of Alexander and his Generals, led the charge, and after a hand to hand combat, in which he received sabre-cut in the mouth and lost several teeth, he had the satisfaction of routing the enemy completely. The main Syrian army now came up and crossed the river. Euthydemus appears not to have risked a general engagement but to have fallen back on his almost impregnable capital. Of the details of the siege we know nothing, but it may be[1] that it is to this blockade that Polybius refers[2] when he says that the 'siege of Bactria' was one of the great historic blockades of history, and a commonplace for poet and rhetorician. Time wore on, and still the "City of the Horse" held out; a long absence from home was unsafe for Antiochus, for the

[1] Von Gutschmid takes this for granted. This is scarcely justifiable.

Syrian Empire might at any moment break out into one of the incessant rebellions which vexed the Seleucids almost without intermission. Both sides, perhaps, were not unready for a compromise, and this was brought about by the good offices of a certain Teleas, a fellow-countryman of Euthydemus, and hence especially suitable for the task. On behalf of the Bactrian prince, he pointed out that it was illogical to cast upon him the blame accruing from the policy of Diodotus II in forming an alliance with Parthia. In fact, Euthydemus was the enemy of Diodotus, and had merited the gratitude of Antiochus in destroying the "*children of those who first rebelled*"[1]. A still more cogent argument sufficed to convince the King. The Scythian hordes were on the move, and threatening the borders of the Jaxartes like a storm-cloud. Bactria was the outpost of Hellenic civilization, and on its integrity depended the safety of the Syrian Empire; and Euthydemus pointed out that to weaken Bactria would be a fatal step for the cause of Hellas; "the Greece land would admittedly lapse into barbarism"[2].

---

[1] *i.e.*, Diodotus, and probably others of the family likely to be in the way. Perhaps, "Antimachus Theos" (see appendix to preceding chapter,) was one of them These words seem to be very strongly in favour of the view that there were two kings of the name of Diodotus.

[2] ἐκβαρβαρωθήσεσθαι τὴν Ἑλλάδα ὁμολογουμένως. Von Gutschmid makes a curious mistake here; taking the passive voice, apparently, for a middle, he says, in his Encyclopædia article, that Euthydemus '*threatened to call in the barbarians and overrun the country.*'

This is the first mention we have of the aggressive attitude of the tribes beyond the Jaxartes :[1] but the problem was evidently not a new one to Euthydemus or to Antiochus. The Seleucid monarch came to the conclusion that it was to his interest to preserve the integrity of this great frontier state, which guarded the roads from India and the North. The terms [2] on which peace was concluded must have caused intense chagrin to the Parthian allies of Antiochus.

An alliance, offensive and defensive, was concluded between the royal houses of Bactria and Syria : this, of course, included the recognition of the claim by Euthydemus to the Royal Title, which was perhaps granted on condition that he should guard the Scythian frontier (for it was chiefly on this ground that the claim had been put forward ;) the alliance, moreover, was to be sealed by the betrothal of the young daughter of Antiochus to Demetrius [3], the gallant prince who had caught the attention of the Seleucid whilst conducting negotiations on behalf of his father in the Syrian camp.

---

1 *Vide* Rawlinson 'Sixth Oriental Monarchy,' p. 58 note

2 For terms, *vide* Polybius XI 34. 9-10. For the whole campaign (except the siege, of which we have been spared no account except the doubtful reference, Bk 29) I have followed Polybius. See also Beven 'House of Seleucus II. 23. ; and Rawlinson *loc. cit.* Date of the treaty, ? 208 B. C.

3 *Ibid* : ' Postremum in societatem ejus admissus."

Euthydemus may have urged on Antiochus the propriety of recovering that old appanage of Bactria, the Satrapy of Parapamisus. The strategic value of the kingdom of Kabul was beyond question ; it had been recognized by Alexander who had placed it in the hands of Oxyartes, who, as we have already seen, probably continued to administer it till by the weakness or negligence of Seleucus Nicator it passed back to the hand of Chandragupta Maurya. It was probably in this domain that Antiochus found the Indian princeling Sophagasenas or Subhagasena reigning ; who the latter was is quite uncertain. It was conjectured at one time that the name Subhagasena is a title of Jalauka, a son of the great Asoka, who had died in 231 B. C.[1] ; but Jalauka himself is a misty personality, of whom we know little besides the vague, though voluminous stories of Kashmir tradition.[2] Euthydemus, on behalf of whom the expedition was mainly undertaken, was under the obligation by the terms of the treaty to provide the means for the expedition. For a third time (the last for many centuries), the tramp of armies from the far West was heard down the long winding defiles of the historic Khyber.

1 First suggested by Lassen, "Indische Alterthumskunde", I think.

Vide Smith, 'Early History of India,' p 171 and 197-8.

But the expedition does not appear to have been carried out with the thoroughness which Euthydemus would have liked. It was little more than a demonstration in force. Subhagasena appears to have yielded very easily, and consented to the payment of a considerable indemnity and the surrender of elephants. Antiochus had already been overlong absent from Syria, and he hastened home by the Kandahar road, through Arachosia and Carmania. Androsthenes of Cyzicus was left behind to receive the sum owing to the Syrian coffers, and to follow with it later.[1]

Euthydemus figures on several fine coins which have been recovered; he appears on them as a man in the prime of life, with a heavy stern face.[2] The wide area over which his coins are found points to a considerable extension of the Bactrian domains. An attempt was probably made in his life-time to annex those territories which had been ceded to Chandragupta by Seleucus Nicator, and with the break-up of the Maurya kingdom on the death of Asoka, this was quite feasible. Doubtless Demetrius took a prominent part in leading his father's armies, and he may have been associated with him in ruling the now extensive dominions of Bactria, though it is probably

[1] ? Circa 206 B. C.

[2] See the illustration, Gard. Plate II.

a mistake to attribute the Indian expedition and the foundation of Euthydemia to this reign. It is, of course, unsafe to draw inferences to certainty from coins, but the coins of Euthydemus [1] have been discovered, not only in Bactria and Sogdiana,[2] but in Parapanisus (which may have been put under the suzerainty of Bactria by Antiochus,) Arachosia, Drangiana, Margiana and Aria.[3] It must, however, be remembered that coins are in circulation long after a monarch's death ; and that it is by no means a foregone conclusion that, because the coinage of a king is found in a particular district, that king ruled the district. Such a discovery merely indicates the wealth and commercial power of the monarch in question ; further inferences may be probable, but if unsupported by external evidence, remain in the realm of probability, and nothing more.

Euthydemus may well have looked back upon his career with pride. By sheer ability he had vindicated his right to the crown he had so violently wrested away. The ablest of the Seleucids had

---

[1] On the obverse we find either a horse (appropriate in the case of Bactria, of Zari-aspa "the City of the Horse,") or the figure of Hercules.

[2] Does this indicate that the Sacae were kept well in hand in this reign ?

[3] "Apollodorus of Artemita says the Greeks (of Bactria) conquered Ariana", if they did, it was probably in this reign or the next (Geo. XI. XI. 1.)

come to punish him as a revolting vassal; before he left, the Bactrian by his dogged valour had won that monarch's respect and friendship. He was lord of a great, fertile and important realm; his son had already shown promise as a warrior and statesman; and the latter's wedding with a princess of the proudest of the Hellenic families, whose royal ancestor, the great "Seleucus the Conqueror," second only to Alexander himself, claimed the God Apollo as his father,[1] was a guarantee of lasting peace and friendship. The hated Parthians were paralysed for the time by their rival's success; and Bactria must have been growing rich in her position at the confluence of the world's trade-routes. Ever since the day when, according to the oft-repeated story, Bindusara sent to request a 'supply of wine and a sophist' from his Syrian contemporary, and Chandragupta sent presents of drugs to Seleucus,[2] the growth of luxury in the Greek world, and the establishment of new cities of the type of Alexandria must have created a great demand for Indian goods. A further proof of the close ties binding India and the West, is found in the fact that, twice at least, Greek ambassadors were in residence at the court of the

1 Laodice said that Apollo was really the father of her son. See Justin XV. 4. q. v.

2 Muller Frag. Hist. Graec: I. 344 and IV. 421.

Mauryas, Magasthenes at the court of Chandragupta, and Deimachus at that of Bindusara.[1]

Frequent as must have been the caravans from the Kabul to Bactria, others doubtless arrived from the distant Seres of the North-East, for the then novel commodity of silk, was in great demand in the luxurious towns of the new and cosmopolitan Hellenic age, of which Alexandria is so typical. The forum of Bactria must have resembled that of Sagala in Menander's days, when traders of every creed and tongue crowded the bazaars and the innumerable shops were loaded with the most heterogeneous articles—muslin and silk, sweetstuffs, spices, drugs, metal work in brass and silver and jewels of all kinds.[2] Small wonder that Euthydemus is regarded as the founder of Bactria : only one storm-cloud marred the otherwise shining prospect, and that was as yet low down on the distant horizon. The barbarians beyond the Jaxartes were still moving uneasily.[3] About the year 190 B. C. the long and eventful reign of Euthydemus came to an end, and the kingdom passed to a worthy successor in Demetrius. Whether Demetrius had already begun his

---

1 Strabo II. 1, 9..

2 Milinda-Prasnya. S. B. E. XXXV. p. 3. *Iron* of a superior quality, was also an important item in commerce with the Seres.

3 If we are to believe the Chinese authorities, the first actual occupation of Sogdiana must have been as early as the reign of Eucratides.

eastern conquests we do not know, but at some period of his reign Bactria reached the climax of her prosperity. The ancient citadel of the Iranians was the capital of a mighty Empire, as the words of Strabo testify:—"The Greeks who occasioned the revolt (*i.e.* Euthydemus and his family), owing to the fertility and advantages of Bactria, became masters of Ariana and India. . . These conquests were achieved partly by Menander and partly by Demetrius, son of Euthydemus. . . . . They overran not only Pattalene but the kingdoms of Saroastos and Sigerdis, which constitute the remainder of the coast[1] . . . . . They extended their Empire as far as the Seres and Phrynoi." Their object, obviously, was to reach the sea for trading purposes,—the same object which led them to secure the high road into China.

The evidence of the coins of Euthydemus (*vide ante*), seems to point to the occupation of Aria by that king.[2] Conquests east of Kabul, on the other hand, appear from Strabo's words to have been the work of Demetrius, probably after his father's death, though this is not certain. Strabo

[1] Geo. XI. XI. 1.

[2] *Demetrius in Anarchosia, vide* Isidorus Characensis, 19, in Muller Frag. Georg. Graec. Min. (vol. I) 1855. When was this town founded? In the reign of Demetrius, or in that of his father? Probably Aria and Anarchosia were subdued simultaneously.

speaks very vaguely of the extent of the dominions of Demetrius. By Pattalene we are to understand the kingdom of Sind, the country which was first taken from Musicanus by Alexander the Great. On the west of the Indus, all the country from the Cophen to the mountains appears to have thus belonged to Bactria: east of the Indus, after the annexation of the kingdom of the Delta (Pattalene), it was not a great step to proceed to subdue the neighbouring kingdom of Kathiawar or Surasthra (the Greek Saraostos). What quite is indicated by the "kingdom of Sigerdis," I am unable to determine. It may have been some minute "kingdom" (*i.e.*, the domain of some petty rajah) between Pattala and Surasthra.

Besides these kingdoms on the coast, we have evidence to confirm the opinion that a considerable portion of the Punjab fell into the hands of Euthydemus as well. It is usual to ascribe to him the foundation of the town of Euthydemia, which he named after his father, according to a not uncommon practice. Euthydemia became the capital of the Bactrian kingdom, east of the Indus, and under its Indian name, Sagala, grew to be a flourishing city of great wealth and magnitude. The question of the identity of Sagala (or

Sakala) is a matter of dispute. It is now held that it is not to be confused with the " Sangala ", razed to the ground by Alexander; and modern authorities identify it with either Shorkot, near the modern Jhang, not far from the confluence of the Acesines and Hydraotes, or Sialkot, further north, near Lahore and not far from the head waters of the Acesines.[1] Later on, we shall see that Menander was born " near Alexandria ", " 200 leagues from Sagala ", and this would certainly point to Sialkot rather than Shorkot, if " Alexandria " is the town at the "Junction of the Acesines and Indus" mentioned by Arrian (Anab. VI. 5). It is difficult to believe that the Bactrians had any permanent hold on the country up to the Chinese borderland.[2] Perhaps all that Strabo means is that all the territory up to the great emporium on the extreme west of Serike, *i.e.*, Tashkurghan in Sarikol, was under Bactrian influence, and, perhaps for commercial reasons, was protected by their troops, from the raids of Sakas and other nomadic marauders.

The coins of Demetrius illustrate the history of his reign in an interesting manner: like his father, he seems to have adopted the god Hercules as his patron deity, and Hercules figures upon

---

1 Smith Early History of India, p. 65 note.
2 See Stein " Sand-buried Cities of Khotan," p. 72.

the coins of Euthydemus and Demetrius,[1] very much as the thundering Zeus figures on those of the Diodoti, or the Dioscuri on the coinage of Demetrius' antagonist and successor, the pro-Syrian Eucratides. These coins were doubtless issued for circulation in Bactria proper, like the famous and striking coin which Gardner reproduces, on[2] which a figure, almost certainly to be identified, the Bactrian Anahid, the national goddess, appears, clad as she is described in the Zend-Avesta.

For use in his domains beyond the Parapanisus, Demetrius issued a series of coins of a more suitable character, remarkable alike for their workmanship and as representing the earliest attempt at that amalgamation of Greek technique and Indian form, which is one of the most striking features of the coinage of the Indo-Bactrian dynasties.[3] To this series we may safely assign the silver coins which represent the King as an Indian rajah, wearing an elephant helmet, and those bearing an elephant's head; these coins are, it must be observed, purely Greek in standard and pattern, and are probably earlier than the series of *square* coins,

---

1 *Vide* Gardner 'Catalogue of Coins of Greek and Scythian Kings,' &c. Plate II. 9 & III. 3: *vide* note 17 *ante*.

2 'Catalogue' III. 1.

3 Do. II. 9 & III. 3.

where an attempt at compromise between Greek and Indian methods first appears.[1]

It seems probable that Demetrius divided his Indian possessions into minor principalities for greater convenience of government; a system of satrapies, or small feudal states, appears to have been the only form of administration found possible by the invaders of India, whether Scythian, Parthian or Greek. It was, indeed, the form of government most adapted to the eastern temperament.; from time to time the influence of some mastermind had consolidated a great Empire; but the bonds had always been purely artificial, liable to dissólution on the appearance of a weak or incapable ruler. It had become apparent on the death of Asoka, how little even the great Mauryas had succeeded in introducing elements of cohesion into their vast and heterogeneous Empire.

The small satrapy appears to have been the natural political unit in India, as the city state was in Greece. However, Demetrius did not arrive at a satisfactory solution of the problem of simultaneously governing two distant and diverse kingdoms. Perhaps his continued absence in India aroused the

---

1 Illustrated by E. J. Rapson in the Gundriss I. 10: Gardner XXX. 3. The inscription is still Greek. Notice the gradual dehellenization, well illustrated by the coinage.

jealousy of the Græco-Iranian kingdom in the North; it may be that the inhabitants of Bactria looked upon Sagala with jealous eyes, as a new and alien capital; at any rate, the absence of Demetrius gave ample opportunity for a rival to establish himself securely in Bactria before the arrival of troops from the far south to overthrow him.

The rival who did this was one Eucratides, Who he was, or what may have been his motive, we can only infer from his coins in a somewhat conjectural fashion; one thing, however, seems more or less plain, that he was connected in some way to the royal house of Seleucus; in his sympathies, and probably by birth, he is distinctly closely bound up with the reigning dynasty in Syria.

Justin implies that he seized the throne about the same time as Mithridates I, *i.e.*, about 174 B. C., or a little earlier: we may suppose that Demetrius was engaged in his Indian conquests and the administrative and other problems they entailed, and either had no leisure to attend to what was happening in Bactria, or did not feel himself strong enough to march against so powerful a rival until his power in the South was sufficiently consolidated. Meanwhile, Eucratides was pursuing a vigorous policy in the North, not always with the success he deserved. Enemies were springing up in all directions to menace Bactria, and Eucratides had to vindicate his right to the throne he had claimed.[1] The first and most formidable rival was Mithridates I. Mithridates appears to have succeeded with the special mission of counteracting Bactrian influence, for Phraotes, his brother, had left the throne to him in preference to his numerous sons, as the ablest successor, and one most likely to continue the great mission of extending Parthian dominion in the East, the progress of which had been thwarted since 206 B. C., when Antiochus the Great had raised her rival to the position of ally and equal. The continual threats of aggression from the Parthians, the ever-increasing pressure on the frontier, which caused various wars (perhaps not of great magnitude, but harássing, as a foretaste of what was to come) on the Sogdian frontier, and a campaign—against whom we are not informed—in Drangiana, made the life of Eucratides anything but peaceful. The struggle with the monarch he had dispossessed, moreover was coming, and Eucratides went to meet it with great spirit. At one time the fortunes of war seemed to have definitely turned against him ; by a final effort

1 *Perhaps Demetrius had left Eucratides in charge of Bactria as Regent.* Some one must have been so left: and this would account for the latter's accumulation of power, his command in frontier wars, etc.

Demetrius, with the huge force of sixty thousand men, caught and besieged his rival, whose army by some means had sunk to only three hundred men. By a marvellous combination of skill and good fortune, Eucratides cut his way out after a siege, which (if we are to believe the only authority upon the incident)[1] lasted five months; and this proved to be the turning point in the war. Soon after, the Indian dominions of Demetrius fell into the hands of Eucratides, and the once powerful Demetrius either perished or was deposed about the year 160 B. C.

If, as is just possible, Eucratides was really the grandson of his royal opponent, the great disparity between their ages would account for the ease with which that once doughty leader allowed himself to be defeated by a handful of desperate men, whom he had conquered with a vastly superior force; it would also save the historian from the necessity of condemning Justin's whole account of these incidents as exaggerated and inaccurate--always a pre-eminently unscientific proceeding in the case of an uncontroverted statement. The victory over Demetrius

1 Justin XLI. 6. tells the story "Though much reduced by losses (in frontier wars) Eucratides, when, besieged by Demetrius King of India, with a garrison of three hundred men only, kept at bay, a blockading force of sixty thousand of the enemy, by continual sorties. Finally, after a five months' seige, he escaped."

is probably commemorated in the fine coins reproduced by Gardner,[1] which represent, in a most spirited fashion, "the great twin Brethren," with their lances at the charge, waving the palms of victory. These were evidently struck for use in Baćtria ; for use in the provinces beyond the Hindu-Kush, very probably he struck a series of coins[2] where the blęnding of Greek and Indian art is illustrated in a curious manner, bearing the goddess Nikê holding a wreath on the obverse, and a Pali inscription on the reverse, in Karosthi characters. The coins are bronze and square, this being another instance in which the Indian shape replaces the Greek circular coin.

It is extremely interesting to notice the manner in which the Greek temperament adapts itself to changed conditions. Eucratides gives himself the title of "Maharajah" [3] (which he translates by the Greek ΜΕΓΑΛΟΥ ΒΑΣΙΛΕΩΣ) in his Indian domains ; in Bactria however he appears as the leader of the Greek, as opposed to the Iranian section of the populace. By birth and leanings it seems evident that Eucratides was thoroughly Greek. His

---

1 *Vide* "Catalogue," plate V. 6-9.

2 Do. VI. 6 & 7.

3 *Raja* seems equivalent to *Chchatrapa*, (satrap) merely, the one being used by the native Indian or Bactrio-Indian petty rulers, the latter, apparently, by the feudatories of Parthia. To render ΒΑΣΙΛΕΥΣ "Maharajah" is required The ΜΕΓΑΣ ΒΑΣΙΛΕΥΣ of some of the coins is an attempt at a "literal" translation of "Maharajah".

coins betray his pride of birth; the distinctive figure on nearly all his Bactrian issues is a representation of the Dioscuri, mounted; they were the patron saints of the Seleucids, and under the rule of the 'son of Laodice', took the same place on his coinage as Zeus, the thunder-god, did on the coins of the Diodoti. One of the most striking features of Bactria is the utter predominance of everything Greek in its history. The coins are essentially Greek, the rulers are certainly so, and often not even naturalized Iranians but foreigners, to all appearances. The Iranian population never seems to have had any voice at all in the government; though we must remember that Greek was the language of commerce and civilization in Western Asia, and we are apt to be easily misled by the fact that Greek names, coinage and language were exclusively used. In Parthia, for instance, we know that national feeling was utterly anti-Hellenic, and yet Greek appears to have been the language generally used for commercial and public purposes. Perhaps it was his love for Greek customs and his pride in his Seleucid blood that brought about the downfall of Eucratides.

While returning from India, Justin tells us, he was murdered by his own son, who had shared the throne with him, and who, far from concealing the murder, declared that he had killed "not a parent, but a public enemy", and brutally drove his chariot through the dead monarch's blood, and ordered his body to be cast out unburied. (Circa 156 B. C.) Thus perished one of the most remarkable of the many really great, though obscure, monarchs of the Bactrian Empire. A splendid coin, figured by Gardner in his Catalogue, enables[1] us to form a very good idea of the appearance of the king—a proud determined man, wearing the *Kausia*, diademed with crest, and the bull's horn at the side. On the reverse, significantly, are figured the Dioscuri, charging with long lances and waving the palms of victory. The delineation of the steeds is worthy of the highest traditions of Greek Art. The title of '*the Great*' appears on the coin; ΒΑΣΙΛΕΩΣ ΜΕΓΑΛΟΥ ΕΥΚΡΑΤΙΔΟΥ* . The name of the parricide who thus foully deprived his father of his life and throne, is not recorded. Some authorities have identified him with Heliocles[2], who is supposed by them to have headed a native reaction, fomented either by his father's Hellenizing tendencies, or by

---

1 Gardner Plate V. 7.

2 Tarn, "Hellenism in Bactria". J. H. S. 1902. p. 272.

* Another coin of this reign is the magnificent twenty-star gold piece, at present in the Bibliotheque Nationale at Paris. It was, as far as we know, by far the largest gold coin struck in antiquity, (Alexander issued two-stakr pieces,) and is in every way unique. It fittingly marks the high water mark of Bactrian prosperity under Eucratides; after this reign it gradually decayed. Bactria is indicated by the fact that only silver and bronze coins have been discovered.

his inactive policy against Mithridates. Mithridates, we know, took the satrapies of "Aspionus and Turiva"[1] from Eucratides, and it is possible that this caused dissatisfaction at the policy of the Bactrian Monarch. There is, however, good reason to suppose that the parricide's name was Apollodotus,[2] who may have been led by the supposed patriotic character of his deed to assume the titles of ΣΩΤΗΡ ΝΙΚΗΦΟΡΟΣ and ΜΕΓΑΣ which we find on his coins. It is supposed that Heliocles avenged his father's murder and secured the throne, probably putting his brother to death; some have thought that this is indicated by the title "ΔΙΚΑΙΘΣ" which appears on his coins. It is probable however that the title of the "Just" is of quasi-religious significance, but the discussion of this point may be more appropriately left for another occasion.

Apollodotus seems to have enjoyed a very brief reign and Heliocles probably succeeded in 156 B. C. With him the rule of the Greeks in Bactria comes to an end, the Bactrian princes were forced to transfer their empire to their capital beyond the Hindu-Kush. The murder of Eucratides was worse than a crime, it was a blunder; the death of the one man capable of saving the situation rendered

[1] Strabo Geog. XI. II. 3. Nothing more is known of them.
[2] Cunningham Num. Chron. 1869, p. 241, &c.

resistance useless, and the country was still further enfeebled by the rise of a number of petty princelings or satraps, who were necessary for the government, as we have seen, of the immensely increased Bactrian territory, but who were always inclined, on the removal of a strong hand to assert the independence. The semi-independent character of these petty rajahs or satraps is shown by the style of the inscriptions upon their coins.

APPENDIX TO CHAPTER IV.

SOME PROBLEMS RAISED BY THE COINAGE OF EUCRATIDES.

1. A coin figured by Gardner ("Catalogue," &c. p. 19) has caused a good deal of trouble to numismatists. Gardner and the older authorities read the inscription on it as KARISIYE NAGARA DEVATA "God of the city of Karisi." The identity of the mysterious "City of Karisi" caused much expenditure of ingenuity. Von Gutschmid identified it with "Charis in Aria" (Encyc : Brit. XVIII. p. 591, footnote, column 1). Rhys Davids, in his introduction to the "Questions of Milinda", showed that it was "philologically possible" to connect it with Kelasi on the Indus, the birth-place of Milinda, Menander? Professor Rapson, however, has shown that the reading on the coin is not KARISIYE but KAVISIYE. This simplifies the problems immensely. "KAVISI" is *KAPIŚA*, the name given to North-Eastern Afghanistan, the country north of the Kabul River. (The word Ki-pin which, under the Han dynasty, means Cashmir in Chinese works, bears the same meaning as KAPIŚA in Chinese

writers of the 7th century. It appears to be the Chinese equivalent of Kapiśa. See V. A. Smith's History Ed. 1, page 220, footnote). The coin in this case was merely struck to celebrate some conquest of Eucratides over the country to the South of the Parapanisus; perhaps it was issued when he had won his great victory over Demetrius, for local circulation to emphasize the change of rulers.

2. A more difficult problem is raised by the series (Gard. Plate VII, 9-10) bearing the inscription:—

It seems fairly clear that Laodicé is a Seleucid princess, and the most reasonable supposition is that she was the daughter of Demetrius by his marriage with the daughter of Antiochus III. This seems fairly probable; and, supposing for the moment we take it for granted, we are confronted by the problem, *who is the Heliocles of the coins?*

Perhaps it would be better to classify the views which have been, or may be, held on the subject—

(a) Heliocles is the son of Eucratides, who afterwards succeeded him. It is possible that after deposing Demetrius, Eucratides attempted to conciliate his rivals by marrying his daughter to a prince of the fallen house, and this policy too might prevent any trouble with the Seleucid Kings. It is noticeable that Laodicé, a princess in her own right, is *crowned* on the coins with the royal fillet; Heliocles, being merely a prince, has no insignia. This seems to fit in with the views of Von Sallet[1] and Von Gutschmid,[2] and others.

(*b*) Gardner however has a strong argument to urge against this view. Can we possibly interpret the inscription in any other way but by supposing the ellipse of the usual ΥΙΟΣ? The view stated above compels us to supply ΠΑΤΗΡ, which would be most unnatural. It seems as if the inscription *must* bear its natural interpretation "Eucratides, *son of* Heliocles and Laodicé," and this view is supported strongly by the fact that the people figured in the coins are both *elderly*, and by the fact that Heliocles is not crowned,—he lived and died a private citizen, though husband of a princess. The theory is further confirmed when we remember that in

---

1 *Vide* "Catalogue," plate V. 6-9.
2 Do. VI, 6 & 7.

Greece it was extremely common to name a child after its grandfather, we are pretty certain that Eucratides had a *son* named Heliocles, and that lends additional probability to the supposition that his *father* was named Heliocles too. If we take it as proved that the persons represented on the coins are the parents of Eucratides,—and the cumulative evidence seems to point most curiously in favour of that conclusion,—we are left to choose between two views, which we will label (*c*) and (*d*) respectively.

(*c*) *Eucratides was the grandson of his rival and predecessor Demetrius through Laodicé, the latter's daughter.* This is a bold view, but may be the true one. Demetrius was married soon after the siege of Bactria, and Laodicé, if she is his daughter, might have been born as early as 206 B. C. But in that case Eucratides, at the earliest, could hardly have been born before 192 B. C.; we have strong grounds for believing that his accession to the throne took place in 174 B. C., as that was the date of the accession of Mithridates; and Justin expressly tells us (XLI, 6, 1.) that they both came to the throne about the same time. But according to this theory, he was only eighteen when he achieved his final victory, and that after a long conflict. This would certainly be a remarkable achievement for a mere boy. Again, if this be the case, we must certainly put back the date of the death of Eucratides, as he certainly could not have had a son old enough to murder him and declare himself king (as described by Justin XLI, 6) in 165 B. C., at which date Eucratides was himself under thirty on this hypothesis. But the date may be wrong.

(*d*) Perhaps the most tenable theory is, that the Heliocles of the coins *is* the father of Eucratides, and Laodicé his mother; but that the latter was *not* the *daughter* of Demetrius by his Seleucid wife, but a relation—sister, cousin, or some such connection—who had accompanied her to Bactria, perhaps, when she was married to the young prince. On the other hand, Laodice is certainly a name which would point to *direct* descent from a Seleucid King (the first Laodicé was the mother of the founder of the dynasty); and a striking point in favour of theory (*c*) is found in the medals of the Agathocles, who will be dealt with in the succeeding chapter. Agathocles apparently issues these medals in commemoration of his royal ancestors, and amongst these (they include Alexander the Great and Diodotus) is one which bears the image and superscription of "Antiochus Nicator". I shall try and show, in a later place, that this is Antiochus III; and if so, it seems that Agathocles traces his descent through a long line of kings back to Antiochus, *i. e.*, that children of Demetrius and his Seleucid wife actually occupied the throne.

(The student is referred to Von Sallet *Die Nach : Alex : der Gross im Bact* : Tarn's article on *Hellenism in Bactria and India* in the *Journal of the Hellenic Society* 1902, and Wilson *Ariana Antiqua*, p. 264 ff.)

CHAPTER V.

THE OVERTHROW OF THE NORTHERN KINGDOM.

SINCE the days when Alexander made his demonstration in force north of the Jaxartes and the town of Furthest Alexandria, built on the uttermost limit of the Greek world, was erected as a frontier fort to keep watch and ward over the barbarians of the Outer Waste, there had been a feeling of vague unrest among the Greeks in the Far East, regarding the likelihood of trouble from the mysterious hordes of the northern steppes.

No one knew their extent or power, which made them all the more formidable; perhaps memories of the terrible Cimmerians of the old days had become a kind of tradition in men's minds; for at all periods of the history of the ancient world we seem to detect a feeling of latent anxiety, a prescience of what was to come, with regard to the vast tribes of "barbarians" who from time to time burst like a sudden cyclonic wave on the barriers of civilization,—feared, because their numbers, power, and resources were only known through vague report and extravagant rumour. The very fact that the Parthians, once an obscure nomadic tribe, pasturing their herds on the grassy slopes between the Oxus and the Ochus, had suddenly thrust into the heart of the Greek world a great anti-Hellenic Empire, proud of its antagonism to Greek ideas, and aggressively eager to dispute with all comers its right to the position of ruling state in Asiatic Greece, was a warning of what the barbarian might do, and of the risk of despising him.[1]

Bactria was destined to be overwhelmed by the operation of the same irresistible force which finally swept the civilization of the ancient world utterly away; obscure hordes on the Mongolian plains, far beyond the ken of Hellenic observation, were slowly but surely pressing south, and the impetus was finally being transmitted to the tribes on the fringe of Hellenic civilization, till at last, by sheer physical pressure, they were driven over the border, sweeping all before them with the force of an avalanche.

Signs of trouble on the northern border had been observed by Euthydemus, and Antiochus the Great had had the wisdom to see the danger of

1 In a previous chapter, I have tried to point out the likelihood of a *Sacaean Helot population* in Bactria—an aboriginal substratum, whose existence points to the constant tendency of the Northern tribes to move southwards and westwards, which had begun before the coming of the Iranians.

weakening Bactria. Other causes however had been at work to drain Bactria of her resources, the constant antagonism of Parthia, and the brilliant but expensive conquests of Demetrius in India, till at last the Bactrian Greeks were literally "drained of their life-blood," as Justin graphically says,[1] "and a comparatively easy prey." Indeed, one of the most striking features of Bactrian history is the wonderful persistence of the Greek element. No Iranian appears to have ruled in Bactria after the accession of Diodotus, and the Greek kings, if we may judge by their coins, were proud of their Hellenic blood, and kept up the best traditions of their national art. Even in the Southern Kingdom there appears at first little evidence that the Greek spirit was likely to be absorbed into its Indian environment; on the contrary, few things are more remarkable than the manner in which the Greek spirit adapts itself to altered circumstances, and blossoms out into a new life, infusing something of the "diviner air" of the old masters into the coins of Menander and his contemporaries, or, later, into the friezes of the Buddhist sculptures of Gandhara.

In the troubled times which followed the death of Eucratides, events occurred which must have

1 "*Exsanguee*" XLI, 6.

finally wrecked any chance Bactria had of offering any effectual resistance to the impending invasion of the Sacae. Heliocles, as we have seen, succeeded Eucratides ; we know very little of him except that his coins invariably bear the inscription ΔΙΚΑΙΟΣ ; it was formerly held that he murdered his father and took this title to assert the justice of slaying a king whom a section of his subjects appear to have regarded as a public enemy. It is more probable, however, that Heliocles was his father's avenger and on that ground assumed the title of the "Just", though the title may merely be a translation of the Buddhist *dharma-kasa*, if indeed Heliocles was influenced by the spread of Buddhism to the extent to which most of his successors appear to have been.

Mithridates, as we have noticed already, had inaugurated the aggressive policy against Bactria for which he had received his crown, in the reign of Eucratides, with some success. If, as it has been asserted, Eucratides lost his life owing to his inability to resist Parthian aggression, his successors were not less deserving of a similar fate. Mithridates continued to advance, and he appears to have actually held Bactria for a time as a sort of vassalage. If we can trust references in Orosius and Diodorus, he even attacked the Southern Kingdom, and penetrated to Euthydemia itself. We may fairly safely infer, however, from the silence of Justin, and also from the fact that no Parthian coins are found over the Parapamisus, that the occupation was not of a very lasting character, and may indeed have only been a demonstration in force, like the expedition of Antiochus III against Subhagasena.[1] Perhaps we may find an echo of these obscure and almost unrecorded campaigns in a Parthian coin which is still extant in the British Museum collection.[2] It represents a standing figure of Hercules, and appears to have been imitated from the coins of Euthydemus II and Demetrius of Bactria.[3]

Fortune however appears to have intervened on this occasion on behalf of Bactria. Demetrius II of Syria had not quite forgotten the claims which Bactria had on the Seleucid house—claims arising from the treaty of Antiochus, and the ties of marriage uniting the two royal families. Between the years 142—136 B.C., he advanced against Parthia, intent on another of the

[1] He appears to have subdued the Sacae princes of Taxila, the kingdom between the Indus and Hydaspes.

[2] Catalogued by Warwick Wroth, Plate III. 7.

[3] Gardner, Catalogue. II 9 and III 3.

many spasmodic efforts of the Syrian Kings to check the growth of their powerful rivals. His army on the march was greatly strengthened by reinforcements from Persia, Elymais and Bactria, and routed the Parthians in a succession of battles.[1] The Parthians, however, maintained the struggle with their usual persistency and finally achieved by stratagem what they were unable to effect by force. Demetrius was enticed to his enemy's camp by pretended overtures and entrapped; he was publicly paraded as a warning to the cities which had joined his standard of the futility of reliance upon Syria.

In the year 136 B. C., Mithridates I died. He was succeeded by Phraotes II, and it was during his reign that the great Sacaen invasion took place, which swept over Bactria with such amazing suddenness and completeness. The movements which led to the great irruption have been worked out with tolerable completeness, chiefly by reference to Chinese authorities; however, it is not proposed here to enter into minute discussions upon the obscure movements of the various tribes, with the many historical difficulties they involve, as the subject is scarcely relevant to the student of the

[1] Justin XXVIII. I. 3, 4.

fortunes of Bactria, and only interests us in so far as Bactria is directly concerned; what happened, appears to have been briefly as follows :—

About the year[1] 165 B.C., the great tribe of the Yuehchi were driven out of their pastures in N.-W. China by a rival horde, and moving in a south-westerly direction came into contact with the conglomerate bands of Scythians, whom the Greeks knew by the vague general name of Sacae,[1] who may be identified pretty certainly with the Sakas of the Indian writers, and the Su, Sai, Se, Sek or Sok of the Chinese Annalists. The Sacae appear to have already settled to some extent south of the Jaxartes; we know nothing for certain about the state of Sogdiana under the Bactrian Kings, but probably, with the extension of the Empire in the south, the Greek hold on the province north of the Oxus became more and more nominal, till it was finally no longer asserted at all.

About the year 136 B.C., after the death of Mithridates, the results of this pressure upon the Bactrians and Parthians began to be seriously felt.

---

1 In a previous chapter I have tried to point out the likelihood of a *Sacaen Helot population* in Bactria – an aboriginal substratum whose existence points to the constant tendency of the Northern tribes to move southwards and westwards, which had been before the coming of the Iranians.

The first omen of the approaching trouble proceeded from a body of Sacae who had enlisted as mercenaries in the army of Phraotes, probably because they had been driven out of their old pasture-lands and had no other occupation. They arrived too late to assist in the war for which they were hired, and being discontented at the treatment they received began to plunder the country. Phraotes, who appears to have been incapable and unpopular, fell in trying to put them down, chiefly owing to the treachery of his Greek forces, who were exasperated by his cruelty.[1]

The Parthians now reverted to the original royal line for a successor to the throne, whom they found in another brother of the elder Phraotes, Artabanus, uncle of the last king. Artabanus appears to have followed these plunderers up; but in a campaign against the Thogarii, says Justin, he was wounded in the arm and died at once,—possibly because the weapon was poisoned. One is strongly tempted to identify these "Thogarii" with the "Tochari", who, together with the "Asii, Pasiani, and Sacarauli",[2] are mentioned by Strabo as being the best known of the Sacaen tribes who crossed the

1 Justin XLII. 1-2.

2 Geog. XI. 8. 2. Von Gutschmidt thinks *all* these names attempt to render "Yuei-Chi" in Greek.

Jaxartes and invaded Bactria.[1] The Tochari appear to have established themselves on a more or less permanent footing in Sogdiana, and so would naturally be the chief opponents of the Parthians. The Sacae appear to have exacted tribute in a most extortionate manner from the people bordering on the country they had overrun, forcing them to pay a certain sum of money on condition that their lands should only be overrun and plundered at certain seasons.[2]

To Heliocles belongs the melancholy distinction of being the last king of Northern Bactria. The Bactrians were indeed little in a fit state to cope with the situation. Their life-blood had been drained by the Indian schemes of preceding kings, and the consequent withdrawal of the more able and adventurous among them to seek a more extended career in the new addition to the Empire; and, as in the case of every nation which has tried to conquer the East without taking the utmost precaution to preserve the integrity of their race from intermixing with the subject stock, the East was

---

[1] In a previous chapter, I have tried to point out the likelihood of a *Sacaean Helot population* in Bactria—an aboriginal substratum whose existence points to the constant tendency of the Northern tribes to move southwards and westwards, which had begun before the coming of the Iranians.

[2] Strabo Geog. XI. 8 3.

gradually absorbing them into itself. As we have already observed, the coins begin to show that Greek standards of thought and manners were gradually becoming less and less carefully adhered to; and on account of the state of Bactria, presumably shortly after the invasion of the Sacæ, confirms the view that Bactria[1] had little that was Greek left in it at the time of its final overthrow. From the annals of Chang-Kien[2] we learn that the Ta-Hia or Bactrians were very like the other tribes between Ferghana and An-Si (Parthia). These people all spoke various dialects, but all understood one another; they were agricultural, treated their wives with an exaggerated respect, and allowed them great liberty, and were all distinguished by deep set eyes and thick beards. They were bad and cowardly soldiers, and only fond of trade.[3] The description of the Bactrians here given by one who was evidently a close and accurate observer, shows fairly conclusively to what extent the process of

---

1 I have not thought it necessary to discuss Bayer's theory that the Greeks were driven out of Bactria by *Parthia*. He misunderstands Justin.

2 Envoy from the Chinese Court to the Yueh-Chi. He returned after various adventures in 126 B.C.

3 Von Gutschmid says it is 'remarkable that Chang notices no difference between the Greeks and their Iranian subjects.' The explanation is simple, there were no pure Greeks left. Some remains of the old Aryan (Iranian not Greek) population may still be traced in the language of the non-Tartar people dwelling round Balkh (Rawlinson, Herodotus, App. Bk. vii., Essay I, p. 207. M. Muller, Languages of the Seat of War, p. 33).

absorption had been going on, and explains what would be otherwise difficult to comprehend—the reason why Bactria succumbed without a struggle worth recording to the incoming flood of invasion. Two brief references are all that Western historians have deigned to devote to the subject, and the inference is that the once famous 'City of the Horse' surrendered without a struggle to the advance of a foe so long threatened that it had lost the terror of novelty; Heliocles and such families as had enough Greek instinct to refuse to dwell under the rule of the illiterate barbarians probably retired before the enemy's advance to their friends on the other side of the Parapamisus. It was far different in the case of the once weaker Parthia, which was able, not only to repair the losses suffered from the Scythian attack but finally to retake part of the old Bactrian territory; so that the poet Horace—with some inaccuracy, it is true, can write—

"*Regnata Parthis Bactra,*"

in an ode which must have been published about the year 25 B. C.

The Barbarian Invasion, then, may be said to have branched off into two distinct channels. The motive force was provided by the advance of the

Yueh-Chi; and this great movement, which ended by the Yueh-Chi occupying the old kingdom of Bactria, forced another great portion of the Sacæ—the Sakas proper, possibly the Sok or Sse of our Chinese authorities, and the Saca-rauli of Strabo—to seek 'pastures new' still further from the borders of their restless and powerful kinsmen. This no doubt caused the Saka irruption into India, though how and when the Saka princes found their way into the Punjab is never likely to be definitely settled. It is usually supposed that they descended into the Ki-pin or Cashmere valley, and from thence gradually spread over the Gandhara district, and finally settled in a series of petty principalities in the Punjab, such as the very flourishing states of Taxila and Mathura (or Muttra) on the Jumna, from which they displaced Native Rajahs. Others even reached the Peninsula of Surasthra, across the formidable Sind deserts, and, together with the Greek invaders already settled in the North-Western corner of India, inaugurated a period which has left behind it some very remarkable traces, both in coinage and architectural remains. There was no contemporary historian to chronicle the brief careers and brilliant courts of the Rajahs of Taxila or Sagala; it remains for us to read the riddle as far as may be, from the evidence which the ravages of time have spared for the ingenuity of the modern investigator.

We have seen that Euthydemus hoped to manage his huge realm upon a kind of feudal plan, which had obtained from immemorial time in the East. Probably one of the earliest of the princes who reigned south of the Parapamisus was one Euthydemus, whom it is convenient to call Euthydemus II; he appears to have been a son of Demetrius, and named, according to the old Greek custom, after his grandfather. His reign, to judge by the paucity of coins, was short; it is probable that he was reigning in the Kabul valley, while two other princes, Pantaleon and Agathocles, were holding small frontier kingdoms on the west bank of the Indus. It is curious to notice, that, while the coins of Euthydemus II indicate that he ruled over a people who had a good deal of Greek blood in their veins, those of his two contemporaries are extremely ungreek in their character. The latter are remarkable for being of nickel, and for bearing inscriptions in the Brahmi instead of the Karosthi script; their general similarity in these respects, and also the fact that both put the bust of Dionysus on their coins, make it seem highly probable that the two princes were closely related in some way ; Pantaleon appears from his portraits to have been the older, and probably Agathocles succeeded him. Pantaleon and Euthydemus were probably contemporaries, and date from some time fairly early in the reign of Demetrius; soon after that king had begun to attempt some definite settlement of his newly acquired domains in the South. We shall probably not go far wrong in dating their accession at circa 190 B. C., and that of Agathocles at about five years later.

With Agathocles we get numismatic evidence of a rather startling quality; in the shape of a magnificent series of medals which that monarch struck, apparently on his accession. Nothing is more remarkable than the manner in which the Greek spirit flashes out in all sorts of unexpected ways in sculptures and coins of these scanty remnants of the great invasion, a couple of centuries after it had flowed over the Kabul and receded again. A petty Indian Rajah, with little, probably, of the Greek blood he boasted in his veins, and perhaps but little acquaintance with the tongue of which he is so proud, can strike medals which have a Hellenic grace which would not shame the best traditions of Greek art, and which, with a curious pride of race, assert the striker's kinship with the heroic founders of the Bactrian kingdom, and the Seleucid monarch who was proud to be their friend and ally. The first of the series[1] is that bearing the portrait of great Alexander "Son of Philip" himself; then comes Diodotus, the founder of the Bactrian Empire, with the title ΣΩΤΗΡ which appears on that monarch's own coins; Euthydemus I[2] with the title Theos, ancestor, no doubt, of the monarch; and lastly Antiochus Nicatôr The latter, it appears, must be none other than Antiochus III, whose daughter married Demetrius. Agathocles is proud of his descent from the Royal Line of Bactria; would he not naturally be far prouder of his connection with the Seleucids, the family which, in spite of two centuries of blundering and misrule, still enjoyed a semi-divine reverence from their subjects, descended, as they claimed to be, from Apollo himself? Gardner and other authorities[3] hold that the very title Nicatôr is against the identification of Antiochus with Antiochus III, who assumes invariably on his extant coins the title of

---

[1] Figured in Gard: Catalogue IV. 1-3. They trace this descent back to Philip of Macedon, doubtless to impress the subject, with their monarch's importance.

[2] Notice the royal fillets, and title Basiluse.

[3] Gardner Cat: Introduction, pp. XXXVIII-IX. Babelone Rois de Syrie. XLII.

ΒΑΣΙΛΕΥΣ ΜΕΓΑΣ. However Gardner himself, quoting "from a passage of Malala",[1] admits that the title appears to have been actually used by Antiochus III, and certainly he would appear most appropriately on Bactrian coins. These coins bear on the reverse the striding Zeus, already familiar to us as the crest of the Diodoti. Two curious coins throw some side-lights upon the policy and tendencies of the smaller Bactrian principalities; on a coin of Pantaleon appears a spirited representation of a Nautch girl, wearing trousers, and depicted as dancing, with a flower in her hair. Whether this was an attempt to conciliate his Indian subjects, or to commemorate a court-favourite, it is impossible for us to tell; the vivid delineation of a typically Eastern subject with something of the grace of the Greek is another landmark in the history of the Hellenic race in one phase of their absorption into the country they had invaded. More remarkable in many respects is the purely Buddhist coin (IV. 10 Gardner) where the Stupa or Dagaba, and the Buddhist Rail are delineated.

There is no doubt that Buddhism took a strong hold on the invaders of India from the North-West;

1 John of Malala, the Byzantine, I., p. 261.
Why *should* Antiochus II appear on Bactrian coins?

indeed the Punjab and the Gandhara district appear to have become the centre of Buddhism in its declining days; of the two most remarkable of the kings of that part of India, the Greek Menander and the Scythian Kadphises I, were Buddhists, the latter ranking next to Asoka himself in the history of the creed of Gautama. The reason is not far to seek; the invaders, quickly settling in the land of their adoption, had none of the prejudices, the conscious desire for isolation, which creates so infinite a gulf between rulers and ruled in the East of to-day; they were ready to adopt the customs and gods of the country, to worship, as the precept of Socrates enjoyed, "after the fashion of the state they dwelt in."

But orthodox Brahmanism had no place for the "Barbarian", the foreign casteless chieftain, who might enter their cities, but never their ranks; Buddhism, on the other hand, had none of the exclusiveness of the Brahmin creed; it boasted, on the contrary, of its disregard of caste, and hence, while ousted from India proper, slowly but surely, by Brahman influence, it retained its hold on Scythian and Greek invaders, and spread to far countries like Ceylon and Japan, and even to the fastnesses of Thibet.

Contemporary, or nearly contemporary, with these princes appears to have been Antimachus Nicephorus,—Antimachus II as he is usually called, to distinguish him from the mysterious prince of that name who appears to have been a rival of Euthydemus when the latter overthrew Diodotus, and to have claimed in some way to be the rightful successor to the throne of the murdered king. It would, then, seem that Euthydemus distributed his Eastern domains among members of his family, probably reserving the capital, Sagala, for himsef and his direct descendants, such as Demetrius, who had actually undertaken the conquest of the East. Among the minor princes of the family of Euthy-demus appears to have been one Strato, husband of Agathoclea, whose coins with their figure of the sedent Hercules, seem to connect themselves with those of Euthydemus.[1] Strato appears to have been succeeded by a son of the same name; one coin of this king shows a strange departure from Greek tradition: Apollo is figured with his hair knotted in a curious queue, somewhat like that affected by the modern Sinhalese.[2] Strato appears to have been a contemporary of Heliocles.

---

1 Compare Gardner's representation XI. 6 with the Euthy-demus type. 1. 11.

2 Gardner XI., 2.

Coins of Heliocles, of the Persian standard, square and with bi-lingual inscriptions, are found in the Kabul valley, and were probably issued after his expulsion from Bactria by the Scythians.

Among this confused mass of petty princes, whose coins are the only evidence for their existence, it is possible to trace out here and there two distinct lines of succession—the feudatories who claimed descent from Euthydemus and those who based their royal rights upon their loyalty to, or kinsmanship with, the usurper Eucratides. To the former group belong Pantaleon, Agathocles, Antimachus II, and Strato, and his descendant of the same name; to the latter, Antialcidas, Lysias and Diomedes. Their coins, except one, bearing the figure of an elephant, figured by Gardner (Cot. VII. 9.) are all bi-lingual, and show unmistakable signs of deterioration from the artistic point of view; they seem to be the work of artists to whom Greek tradition is little more than a meaningless form, and are mostly bad copies of the Dioscuri type of Eucratides.

The frequent recurrence of the Dioscuri on these coins lead to the opinion that the princes who struck them wished to intimate their association with the house of Eucratides. Lysias, too, appears wearing the "Kausia" or highland bonnet which was, as we have already mentioned, affected by Eucratides.[1] Perhaps Plato, whose coin dates itself at 165 B. C., was the first of this line. To proceed further, however, with the list of minor rulers of whose achievements even their coins can teach us little, is useless to all practical purposes ; it is now necessary to turn to the history of those Saka chieftains who were settled side by side with the Greeks in the Punjab and the surrounding districts. In all probability they had entered India from the North, as already related, passing through the country of the Byltai (little Thibet), into Ki-pin or Cashmere, and thence down the Indus. The Sakas who entered India are no doubt those Sai-Wang (princes of the Sai), whose defeat is mentioned in the 9th chapter of the Han annals.[2] Even before this one body of the Sse had settled in the valley of the Cophenes, which they found an easy conquest owing to the raid of Mithridates I. (c. 160 B. C.) Two important towns sprang into importance as centres of Saka rule: the first (and doubtless the oldest, situated as it was in the country into which the Sakas first entered), was the town of Taxila on the Cashmere border-land ; the second, far in-

---

1 Gardner XI., 7.

2 Buhler. Ep : Ind : I 36.
Also Inscription "*P*" from Lion Capital.

land, was the great city of Mathura or Muttra on the Ganges, between which and the other Saka States lay various hostile principalities, Greek and Indian. The earliest of the Satraps of Mathura, of whose date we have any clue, appears to have been a certain Rajavula, whose later coins appear to imitate those of Strato II. This would enable us to fix his date roughly at about the year 120 B. C. Now Rajavula succeeded two Satraps, Hagana and Hagamasha, whose predecessors appear to have been Native Indians, to judge by their names; hence we feel justified in placing the occupation of Mathura at about a generation before the accession of Rajavula. Mathura was very probably occupied at a later date than Taxila, although coins give us no support in their view, the first known Satrap of Taxila being the Liaka Kusuluka of the "Taxila grant"—the inscription engraved on a metal plate, which has been found in the neighbourhood of the modern city. The Sakas are also mentioned (unless the reference is to "Sakya", *i. e.*, Sakya-muni, a title of the Buddha), in an inscription at Mathura, commonly dated at about 100 B. C. or earlier.

The most remarkable, and from many aspects inexplicable, fact, is that these "Satraps", as their very title implies, are subordinate in some way to

Parthia. The only explanation that can be offered is, that the Sakas were in occupation of the Taxila country somewhat earlier than the time when we first find traces of their settlement there, and that Mithridates in his Indian expedition actually annexed the old kingdom of Porus, as Von Gutschmidt infers.[1] "The kingdom of Porus" included the nations between the Indus and the Hydaspes, and would also include the princes of Taxila, who would henceforth be content with the title of "Satrap", which it is improbable they would otherwise assume, it being the custom with their neighbours to assume a style, the grandeur of which appears to be in inverse proportion to the size of the petty realms they governed. Mithridates appears to have exacted an allegiance which was more or less nominal; however, as there are no traces of a permanent Parthian occupation south of the Hindu-Kush, and Justin (41, 6, 8) expressly names this range of mountains as the limit of his kingdom to the East.

Probably this invasion of India took place soon after the death of Eucratides, and, with the death of the great Parthian monarch himself, no doubt the hold of Parthia on the Saka princedoms became

[1] From Orosius V. 4 and Diod. Sic. p. 597.

more and more a nominal matter, till about the year 120 B. C., or perhaps some twenty years later, a very remarkable personage, whom we may conveniently call by the name of Moga, established himself as an independent monarch at Mathura, and assumed the overlordship of the Saka kingdoms of the Punjab and the Kabul valley. He assumes the very title which their former overlord Mithridates had vaunted, that of "Great King of Kings", and appears to have been looked upon as the founder of a new Era.[1] The copper-plate inscription from Taxila, shows that the rulers of that principality willingly acknowledged the overlordship of Moga. "Patika, son of the Chatrapa Liaka Kusuluka", it reads, "re-enshrined a relic of Buddha, the Stupa of which was in ruins.........in the 78th year of the fifth day of the month Panemus, of the Maharajah Moga the great (Maharajasa Mahantasa Mogasa)." No coins, however, of this "great" king have been found, bearing the name Moga; this would be in itself a very remarkable fact, but the difficulty is solved by identifying Moga with the Maues or Mauas (we only know the name in its genitive form MAYOY), of whose coins we have a consider-

[1] See Fleet's Articles J.R.A.S. 1905, p. 155, and Oct 1907. Also V. A. Smith J.R.A.S, 1903, pp. 46—58; F.W. Thomas J.R.A.S.B. B., 1906. The date of Maues is fixed by Dr. Bhandarkar at 154 A. D. J.B. Br. R.A.S., 20. p. 292 ff. For Maua-Kes compare Arsa-Kes.

able number. That the Saka name Mauakes was well known, and held by the chiefs of the race at one period at least, we know from Arrian, where we find that a leader of that name commanded the Saka contingent of archers at Gaugamela. Recent researches have proved that—Kes is a common "Kose-suffix", and is frequent in the form—gas. Hence Mo-ga or Maua-kes is very probably the Mau-es of the coins; and indeed it would be extremely difficult to account for many circumstances (particularly the total absence of coins of "Moga *the great*", amid the many specimens of minor princes which have come down to us) on any other hypothesis.

In the meantime, the Greek kingdoms were engaged in numberless petty wars: very seldom does the same name appear twice, and never more than twice, in the coins of these petty rulers, and from the dates, as far as we can determine them, it appears that frequent and often violent changes in the succession, took place with great frequency; no less than twenty-three names occur in the space of a century,—the century after the conquests of Eucratides, and an Indian authority speaks of the "fiercely-fighting Yavanas", and mentions that "there was cruelly dreadful war among them; they did not stay in Madhyadesa ".[1] An echo of some forgotten war, perhaps against a Greek neighbour, perhaps against the Saka princes of Taxila, is commemorated in a brilliant series of coins of Antimachus (Gardner V., 1-3) in which Poseidon is figured with the palm of victory. Antimachus had won some naval victory, possibly fought on the broad Indus, with a rival flotilla, striving to effect a landing with troops in his domains. One great king, however, arose, whose power was sufficient to enable him to knit together the warring states into something like a consistent whole; his brilliance, piety and valour are recorded in brief scraps of information which testify in themselves to his power, for he is the only Greek king of the period who has left a mark upon contemporary literature at all. This was Menander, to whom we shall devote the succeeding chapter. Menander appears to have not only consolidated the Greeks into something like a coherent mass, but to have pushed the Scythians of Taxila and Mathura back to the bounds of their original domains, while the mysterious Scythian settlements of Surasthra and the lower Indus—an independent branch of the nation, an overflow, perhaps, of the settlers in

---

1 Gargi-sanhitated Kern, p. 57.

Sacastene, quite separate from the tribes who entered from the north—were apparently subdued altogether.

The stupendous achievements of Menander, however, were only a transitory flash of brightness in the slowly settling gloom, which was gradually overtaking the Indo-Greek peoples.

CHAPTER VI.

FROM THE ACCESSION OF MENANDER TO THE FINAL EXTINCTION OF GREEK RULE IN THE EAST.

THERE is something of the glamour of romance in the dim and half-recorded history of the greatest of the Greek rulers in Northern India. Years after the iron heel of Rome had crushed out of existence the last flickering fires of Greek independence in far-off Hellas; after Alexander's attempt to revive the memories of Marathon and Salamis in a great Greek world-empire had been relegated to the limbo of forgotten and unfulfilled aspirations; in an alien land, under a tropic sky, we still find an individual, endowed with some of the old spirit of his ancestors, and actually building up a great empire of the most heterogeneous elements. Menander went nearer, perhaps, than any of his predecessors, to the accomplishment of Alexander's ideal of welding East and West together, for he alone is enshrined among the heroes of history in the literature of both. Strabo speaks of the greatness of his achievements, and Plutarch points a moral from his piety and posthumous renown; while (though he is forgotten in the land that he once ruled) he lives still in the literature of the distant countries, where Buddhism still exerts an influence; in Ceylon, Siam and Burma the answers which the sage Nagasena gave to the "Questions of King Melinda" are still regarded as authoritative pronouncements on obscure points of doctrine and metaphysics in the teaching of the Buddha. Such is the strange irony of history; for an account of the last of the ancient Greeks who exerted any considerable independent power, we depend upon legends enshrined in the sacred books of an alien creed and tongue, not even preserved in the country where he reigned. Surely no stronger testimony to the power of Greek thought and influence could be found in the pages of history than this—a Greek monarch is found figuring as an important personage in the history of Buddhism; perhaps it is only paralleled by the almost more startling fact that the Buddha himself was once canonized by the Catholic Church, and may still be seen, under the title of 'San Giusafato' in a niche of the cathedral of Palermo.[1]

The dates of the reign of Menander are a matter of great uncertainty. It seems almost im-

1 *Buddha and Baarlam and Josaphat.*—Max Muller. "Chips from a German Workshop." (1875, Vol. IV., pp. 177-189.)

possible to conceive that his reign coincided with that of the powerful Saka line of monarchs, from Maues to Gondophares, for Maues evidently held considerable power; and, as we have seen in the preceding chapter, not only annexed to the kingdom of Taxila and the old kingdom of Porus (the strip of land between the upper reaches of the Jhelam and the Chenab), but also controlled the Saka kingdom of Mathura. To judge by his coins, Azes I was a monarch of considerable power and ability too, though how he succeeded in evolving a powerful and prosperous state out of the wild and rocky tracts of land which constituted the main portion of his realm, is one of the many unsolved problems of the history of the time.[1]

Von Gutschmid puts his date at 125—90 B.C., and says that Menander forced the Saka Empire back within its original bounds. This he infers

---

1 *Coins.*—Gardner catalogues seventy-four of Menander. As compared to other Greek kings, this is the highest; Eucratide coming next with sixty-two. But this is small compared to the number of coins of Azes in the British Museum. Of them, Gardner catalogues over two hundred; but we cannot draw any infallible conclusions from this. V. A. Smith catalogues ninety-five coins of Menander in the Calcutta collection. Over twenty different types have been distinguished; the figure of Pallas appearing, in different form, on the most numerous types.

Rhys Davids says (p. XXI) that the bulk of the coins are "clearly Pagan, and not Buddhist." This is not correct; the coins nearly all appear to have been struck in commemoration of military achievements, and all or nearly all, might have been issued by any king, Buddhist or Pagan, with a strong tincture of Greek culture, who wished to emphasize the importance of his conquests.

from the 'lack of unity' in the later Saka coins; this date however clashes with the most generally accepted era assigned to Maues, who is held by the majority of scholars to have established an independent kingdom in Ki-pin soon after the death of Mithridates I, in the troubled times which followed, until finally Mithridates II repaired the damage done during the reigns of his two predecessors and began to regain the lost ground once more. It seems probable that the date of the accession of Maues was about the year 120 B.C.; and if the usual interpretation of the mysterious "year 78 of the great-king, Moga the Great," is correct, he was still reigning in 99 B.C. over an extensive tract of country.

If, then, we follow Von Gutschmid, we can only conclude that Menander reigned considerably after this; but the most reasonable conclusion is, that his reign was over before Maues consolidated the Saka kingdoms; it seems most probable on the whole that he ruled somewhere between the years 165—130 B.C., and it was only after his death that Maues and his successors held the paramount position in N.-W. India. Their final overthrow was no doubt due to the advance of the Kushans, and had nothing to do with any Greek extension of power.

We have evidence that leads strongly to the hypothesis that the invasion and partial conquest of the old Maurya kingdom took place about the year 155 B.C., Menander was the only Greek who was ever in a position to have made such an invasion, as both his coins and the testimony of Hindu writers lead us to assume.

A passage in the "Questions of Melinda" (III. 7, 5) gives us the traditional account of the birthplace of King Melinda...Menandor, which should enable us to locate it, and also to identify the great city of Ságala. Unfortunately, however, the figures do not yield satisfactory results. "In what district, O King, were you born?" asks Nagasena. "There is an island called Alasanda, it was there I was born." "And how far is Alasanda from here (Ságala)?" "About two hundred yojanas..." "In what town, O King, were you born?" "There is a village called Kalasi," replies the King, "it was there I was born..." "And how far is Kashmir from here?" "About twelve yojanas." So, according to the author of the Questions, Menander was born at the village of Kalasi, on the island of Alasanda, two hundred yojanas from Ságala, while Ságala, the royal capital, is twelve yojanas from Kashmir.

It was formerly proposed to identify Kalasi with the supposed Karisi of the coins of Eucratides ; but it has now been shown that this reading is wrong and Karisi does not exist. The most probable solution appears to be that "*the island of Alasanda*" is none other than the town of Alexander on Indus, the building of which is recorded by Arrian (Anab. VI. 14, 15), at the junction of that river with the Acesines. The town may have been built on some island at the confluence of the two great streams (close to the modern town of Utch), and the name may, in a corrupt form, pass from the city to the island on which it stood.

But a serious difficulty arises here. The birth-place of Menander was two hundred yojanas from Sâgala. Whatever may be the length of the yojana [Rhys Davids says seven miles ; Dr. Fleet would give the Magadha or Buddhist yojana the length of $4\frac{6}{11}$ miles only (J.R.A.S. 1906, p. 1012)], it is impossible to reconcile this measurement with any of the suggested identifications of the ancient Sâgala—Sialkot, Chuniot or Shahkot. Taking the length of the yojana at its most moderate computation, $4\frac{1}{2}$ miles or rather less, we get a distance of 900 miles. No town nine hundred miles from Utch is in the least likely to be identified with

Ságala. The towns mentioned above are less than half the distance away. It is of course quite possible that the Pali word *Dvipa* means "Peninsula" and not "island," and that the town of Kalasi on the piece of land, island or peninsula, called Alasanda, may have to be sought at the mouth of the Indus or on the adjoining coast. In any case Alasanda seems to be a corruption of Alexandria, perhaps some town founded during Alexander's retreat.

We must abandon this puzzling problem, and continue to examine the remaining facts with regard to Menander's career. Very striking evidence is afforded by the vast number and wide distribution of the coins of Menander, of the extent and prosperity of his empire, and the length of his reign from Gujarat to Mathura, in the Kabul Valley and as far north as Cashmir, they have been unearthed in great quantities; the Calcutta collection contains ninety-five specimens alone, and seventy-four are catalogued among the coins in the British Museum. The king appears to have been a relation of Demetrius if we may judge from a certain similarity between the coins of the two kings. The goddess Pallas appears to have been the favourite deity of the monarch as she appears on eighty-four out of the ninety-five coins of Menander catalogued by Smith. However, the Hercules which appears in a British Museum specimen (Gard: XIII. 6) is similar to the 'Hercules' type of Demetrius, while the elephant on the square bronze coin of Menander (XII. 6 Gard.) reminds us of the elephant with a bell attached to its neck, which appears on a round bronze coin of Demetrius (III. 2). Menander appears to have chosen Pallas as the favourite emblem for his coinage, because the warrior-goddess was most appropriate to a great general and conqueror. She appears in various attitudes: sometimes she is hurling the bolt at the king's enemies (Gard. XI. 8—12); sometimes she appears in her casque, while on the reverse, victory holds out a wreath to the conqueror of India (Gard. XI 13 and XII 1.) The king himself is generally represented wearing his helmet, spear in hand. His features are coarse, and appear not to be those of a man of pure Hellenic descent.

Other interesting coins throw a little light upon the vexed question of Menander's Buddhist tendencies; on one (Gard. XII. 7) appears the "wheel of the Law," the "Dharma-chakra," a favourite emblem (see Cunningham, Coins of Ancient India, p. 101, c.).

Others contain interesting inscriptions which may testify to the king's Buddhist leanings; these coins, which are of the square Indian pattern, and are of bronze, have a Pali inscription on the obverse, and its Greek equivalent on the obverse; the question, however, naturally arises, whether the Pali is a vernacular translation of the official Greek inscription or *vice versa.*

In one instance, this certainly appears to be the case. The Pali inscription

Maharajasa Tradatasa Menandrasa

"(coin of) the Maharajah Menandra, the saviour," appears to be nothing more than a literal translation of the Greek motto ΒΑΣΙΛΕΩΣ ΣΩΤΗΡΟΣ ΜΕΝΑΝΔΡΟΥ. The epithet "*tradatasa,*" perhaps a shortened form of *tranadatasa*, is evidently the Pali equivalent for the Sanskrit *trānakatri*, a "saviour."

But is the inscription to be found on the coin described by Wilson (Ariana Antiqua, p. 287, No. 16) and Gardner (p. 50, No. 74) to be reckoned in the same category? Here we have a Greek inscription—ΒΑΣΙΛΕΩΣ ΔΙΚΑΙΟΥ ΜΕΝΑΝΔΡΟΥ.

The Pali inscription on the obverse reads

Maharajasa Dhramakasa Menandrasa

the question naturally arises, is the word "dhramakasa" (or "dharmakasa") a more translation of the corresponding Greek word, or is it to be taken in its natural sense, to mean "one who follows the 'Way,'" *i.e.*, the Law of the Buddha?

It seems to be an extremely elaborate and clumsy rendering of the simple Greek epithet, and it would be far more obvious to consider the Greek word to be a translation of the Pali, and not, as Rhys Davids supposes, the reverse. The Greek language does not contain an exact equivalent for the Buddhist conception of *dharma*, and it would be the obvious course for them to adopt the ready-made equivalent ΔΙΚΑΙΟΣ, first used by Heliocles.

It may be, of course, that the word "Just" had acquired a distinctly Buddhist connotation in the process of contact with a new religion, just as words acquired a new significance when Greek became the vehicle for the expression of an entirely fresh set of conceptions under the influence of Christianity.

We have seen, however, that Buddhism had an extremely strong hold upon north-western India, intensified, perhaps, by the Brahminical reaction which overtook the kingdom of Magadha, when in 184 B. C., Pushyamitra Sunga usurped the throne of the Mauryas, and began to show signs of hostility to the liberal and unorthodox tenets of his predecessors, probably very largely from motives of policy. Nor was Menander the first of the Bactrians to show signs of leaning towards Buddhism. The coins of Agathocles contain one remarkable specimen, (Gard. IV., 10), which has on the obverse the figure of a Buddhist dagaba or stupa, and the "Buddhist rail."

Now Agathocles uses the title of the "Just" on his coins; this may be a mere coincidence, as the same epithet is also applied to themselves by Heliocles, Archebius, Strato and Zoilus, and in the case of the first of these, at least, it is claimed that it was employed by that king as the avenger of his father's murder; the balance of probability, however, is in favour of the theory that, if not actually converts themselves, they were at least strongly influenced by Buddhism, and used the epithet with a distinctly Buddhist significance, to meet the views of their subjects. Finally, the word 'dharma' may be deciphered on a legend of a coin of the last of the Bactrian Greeks, Sy-Hermaeus. Now this coin was issued by Kadphises I in all probability, and it is extremely likely that he was a Buddhist; for his successor, Kanishka, was one of the great figures of Northern Buddhism. We may take it, then, broadly speaking, that the presence of the word 'dharma,' on certain coins of Menander, is not in itself convincing evidence that Menander embraced Buddhism. It does, however, point to the presence of Buddhists among the peoples over whom Menander ruled; and it has been already pointed out that Buddhism was calculated to recommend itself pre-eminently to the casteless foreign invader anxious to adopt the religion of the country in which he had settled, but repelled by Brahmin exclusiveness.

Probably, too, this tendency was strengthened by the revival of Hinduism by the Nandas, the rivals and natural foes of Greek and Kushan alike; it is true, indeed, that by the second century A. D. orthodox Hinduism had re-asserted its influence, but prior to the accession of Kadphises II, it is highly probable that the influence of Buddhism in the North-West has been a good deal underestimated.

In the case of Menander, we have, besides the rather inconclusive evidence of his coins, the tradition embodied in the "Questions," of his conversion. Scholars still dispute the value of this tradition; but it is hardly likely that the writer, who evidently lived in Northern India and was acquainted with the country which Menander once ruled, would have made a statement about a monarch of such renown, unless it were suggested by previous rumours to the same effect, bound up with popular legends about the great rajah of the Yonakas, whose rule in Ságala was not likely to be easily forgotten?

But perhaps the strongest inference as to Menander's Buddhist leanings, may be drawn from a passage in Plutarch, which confirms a statement in the Siamese version of the "Questions" in a sufficiently extraordinary manner. By what strange coincidence, Plutarch should have come in contact with a tradition which appears to have been otherwise only extant among the Siamese Buddhists, it is futile to enquire, but such testimony from two independent sources, so widely separated, is necessarily of high value. One version of the Question (in a passage which has been sometimes considered to be a later addition), states that Menander was not only converted to Buddhism, but, like Asoka, took orders as a Bikkhu, and finally attained to the degree of Arahatship. This tradition (which, as a note in the Sinhalese MS. informs us, was derived from Siam), agrees with Plutarch's account of the funeral of Menander, in his tract "*Reipublicae*

Gerendae Praecepta," page 821, which is as follows :—

> "A certain Menander, ruled with equity among the Bactrians, and died in the field during a campaign. The states, in other respects, joined together in celebrating his obsequies, but over his relics a dispute arose among them, which was, after some difficulty, settled upon the following terms. Each was to take back an equal share of his ashes, that memorials of the Man might be set up among them all."[1]

Mr. Rhys Davids has pointed out the similarity of this account of Menander's obsequies with that

---

1 The passage from Plutarch is quoted in full in the Num. Chron. 1869, p. 229.

The parallel passage in the Maha-Parinibbana-Sutta, Ch. VI., 51-57. (S.B E. XI, pp. 131-133) runs as follows :—"Then the King of Magadha.........sent a messenger, saying......... "I am worthy to receive a portion of the relics of the Blessed One. Over the remains of the Blessed One will I put up a Sacred Cairn, and in their honour will I celebrate a feast.........The Blessed One belonged to the Soldier Caste and I too am of the Soldier Caste." There were seven other claimants, who made application on the same grounds, *i. e.*, that they too were Kshattriayas, like the Buddha. As in the case of Menander, a dispute arose, which was settled by 'Dona the Brahman,' who pointed out that :—

'Unseemly is it that over the division
Of the remains of Him who was the best of beings,
Strife should arise, and wounds and war.

'Ultimately, the relics were divided into eight parts.

'Thus, the writer concludes (62 fin.) 'There were eight Stupas for the relics.'

It is curious to notice that among the recipients were "the citizens of Gandhara." The spread of Buddhism to the North-West began earlier than is generally recognized. The Gandhara district is still to a great extent unexplored as far as the archæologist is concerned. Probably some of the Stupas are of considerable antiquity.

given in Mahaparinibbana Suttana (S.B.E. XI. 133) of the funeral of the Buddha himself; nor does it seem probable that such a dispute for the relics of the dead king would have taken place unless he had, at the time of his death, been commonly regarded as having attained to the degree of Arahatship; and the mention of "relics," and of "memorials," which were to enshrine his ashes, gives the whole account a distinctly Buddhist character. The "memorials" were doubtless the dagabas or stupas, which abound in Buddhist countries, from the Peshawar district to Anuradhapura in Ceylon. It may even be that some of the innumerable stupas which dot the Gandhara district originally contained relics of the greatest of the Indo-Greeks,

---

The reference (53) to the claim of the "Sakyas of Kapilavatthu" (Buddha's own clan) is also worthy of notice. In this connection it may be useful to notice, in connection with the spread of Buddhism among the Sakas, that Buddha himself has often been considered by scholars to have been a Saka by origin himself. The tribe was that of the "Sakyas", their chief town, 'Kapila-vattu' or 'Kapila vastu' is probably *Nagar-Khas* N. W. P. (Cunningham, Anc. Geog Ind., p. 415, 1871 edn) and the Stupa seems to be Scythian in origin; it may have been copied from such models as the conical tents of the Tartars of Kirghiz: also see Herodotus IV. 71, 72, 127 and his account of Scythian tombs. This may account, partly, for the easy assimilation of Buddhism by the later Scythians (Azes, Kaniska etc.)*

* Beal in an interesting article (J.R.A.S., New Series, Vol. XIV, p. 39), shows that the "*Vaggi of Vesale*", who also received relics, were probably none other than the '*Yue-chi*'. This is further proved by the fact that some people on the Sanchi sculptures, who are almost certainly the Vaggians, are by their dress and appearances, *Scythians*. If we can conclude that the Sakyas, the tribe to which Gautama belonged, were Turanians, and closely allied to the Vaggi (*i.e.* Yue-chi and Kushans) we can explain many puzzling problems both with regard to the Buddha himself and also with regard to the spread of Buddhism in the N.-W. of India.

though those opened by Masson early in the nineteenth century, dated chiefly from the time of Azes and his successors, to judge by the coins.

This tradition seems to be the strongest evidence of all for Menander-Milinda's conversion to Buddhism. There is, perhaps, one inconsistency in the story, which has hitherto escaped unnoticed. Was it possible, according to Buddhist tenets, for a warrior, who actually died in the field, to have attained to the supreme degree of spiritual insight here attributed to him? Shedding of blood was always a violation of the law of the Sakya-muni, and Asoka's extreme scrupulousness are a matter of common knowledge. It is in this doctrine that Brahminism and Buddhism are most sharply divided.[1] Von Gutschmidt, though he is not inclined like Rhys Davids, to reject the story of the conversion of Milinda altogether, as based on insufficient evidence, compares the account given by Plutarch with the struggle for Alexander's bones among the "Diadochi." Political and pious motives may have been mingled.

We have the testimony of Plutarch as to the mildness of the rule of Menander; what he says is

---

1 This is scarcely correct; *ahimsā* is one of the few debts to Buddhism which Hinduism acknowledges freely.

further confirmed by the author of the "Questions," who preserves many traditions of the mighty monarch—just, merciful and pious, combining with his warlike characteristics, a reputation for clemency, and a truly Hellenic love of knowledge and philosophic debate. He appears to have kept up the traditions of his adopted religion with a piety which was remembered. "He was a faithful observer," we are told, "of all the various acts of devotion enjoined by his own sacred hymns"; and not less remarkable is the description of Sagala at the height of its prosperity, with its ramparts and towers, its market places, where the wares of all the world were for sale, its mansions rising—a glory of white marble, high into the air, like the snow-capped peaks of the Himalayas. The streets resounded, (and how true to the character of the Greek is this!) with cries of welcome to teachers of every creed, and the city was the resort of the leaders of every sect. In the midst, moated and white-walled, rose the royal citadel, and the yellow robes of the Bikkhus, come to reason with the monarch, flitted like lamps among the snowy colonnades. "In the whole of Jambudipa," the author goes on to say, "there was none comparable to Milinda Rajah, . . . he was endowed with riches and guarded by military power in a state of the utmost efficiency."

Under these circumstances, it is not surprising that a man of Menander's ability and ambitions should soon begin to aspire to emulate the deeds of the great king who had preceded him.

Strabo (XI, 1) goes as far as to consider him greater, in some respects, even than Alexander himself; he quotes Apollodorus of Artemita as his authority for asserting that Menander recovered the Indian conquests of Demetrius (which had, as we have seen, been split up into a number of petty Satrapies, by Greek and Saka princes,) and united them into a single kingdom. His rule, the same authority tells us, extended, as that of Demetrius had done, to the kingdom of the Seres and Phyrni, (which must imply that Menander, for a time, at any rate, held a suzerainty over the Saka settlements in Ki-pin and the valley of Cophen) and extended southwards, not only including Pattalene, but the kingdoms of Surashtra and the neighbouring state of Sigerdis. Perhaps it was with reference to the empire of Menander in the height of its power, and not to the earlier kingdom of Bactria proper, that Apollodorus made the oft-quoted remark that "Bactria is the pride of all Ariana."

The permanent kingdom of Menander no doubt consisted of Punjab, the Kabul valley and the Scinde and Guzarat districts; but his most remarkable achievement was his meteoric advance eastwards, right up to the gates of the historic capital of the Mauryas, which he even appears for a time to have held.

Strabo mentions somewhat doubtfully that Menander is said "to have crossed the Hypanis in his eastward march, and to have reached (the) Isamus." The Hypanis has been variously identified with the Sutlej and the Hypasis or Bias, while "Isamus" has caused much tribulation among critics; it has been variously amended to "Imaus," (referring, it is conjectured, to Menander's penetration into Cashmir) or to "Iomanes" or Jumna, which is also mentioned by the elder Pliny (N. H VI., 21, 7). Others again have preferred to read, "Soanus," the Sona, or to identify the "Isamus" with the Sambus of Arrian (Indica, 4, 4.). The importance of the controversy is almost entirely an academic one; all the rivers mentioned in these conjectures were probably crossed by Menander in his raid on Pataliputra; it seems probable that Cunningham's reading of "Sona" for "Isamus" is right. The Sona flows into the

Ganges, at present a little to the west of the city of Pataliputra; but a former course has been traced, which entered the main stream directly opposite the town. In that case Apollodorus would be justified in saying that Menander went "as far as Soanus"; far east of Pataliputra he probably did not penetrate.

Perhaps the date of Patanjali, the Hindu grammarian, can be now considered definitely settled. The latest theory is that he wrote about the year 150 B. C., and as he was a contemporary (as is evident from his writings) of Menander, we are justified in assuming that Menander's Indian invasion took place at the date now generally assigned to it between the years 155-153 B. C. Pushymitra Sunga had by this time established himself firmly on the throne he had usurped, and it was probably somewhat earlier in his reign that his first conflict with Yavanas took place. Perhaps the first collision between the two powers was that which occurred over the possession of the Sacred Horse, so vividly described in the *Malavikagdimitra*, when a squadron of Greek cavalry actually tried to capture the sacred animal, but were driven off by the young Vasumitra and his detachment of a hundred Rajputs. The '*Asva-medha*' was in itself a challenge to all rivals, as the fact that the horse was able to wander for a year unmolested by any other claimant of the throne, was considered symbolical of the paramount power of the sovereign who dedicated it; and no doubt the gauntlet was readily taken up by Menander's cavalry, though in this instance with ill-success. The conflict took place on the right bank of the Sindhu river, and the Yavana troops were no doubt part of the army investing the town of Madhyamika, near Chitor. The trifling check here inflicted in no way affected Menander's progress; Rajputana, Oudh and the country on both banks of the Jumna (as far north as the Ganges), including the historic Mathura, submitted to the conqueror, who appears to have even reached the gates of Pataliputra.

Menander's empire at its height included an enormous area. Its extent may well have evoked the incredulity of Strabo, for, as he says:—"*if* Menander really reached the Soanus, he must have conquered more nations than Alexander." We may briefly describe his kingdom at its largest extent as being bounded on the south and south-east, roughly speaking, by the Namada and Son rivers; on the north by the Ganges (to its source) and the Himalayas; while on the west, it included a good deal of country on the further side of the

Indus, the Kabul valley, and perhaps all the eastern portion of Arachosia and Gedrosia, from the Cophen river and the Parapamisus to the sea. How it was that Menander never came into collision with his great contemporary, Mithridates I of Parthia, is one of the many puzzling problems of the period. The invasion of India by Mithridates must obviously have taken place before Menander's days, probably before the year 161, when the Sse entered the Cophen valley and "occupied the very site of the Parthian conquests." The occupation of Magadha did not last long; as usual, internal discord arose among the Greek princes of the Punjab, which forced Menander to abandon his claims to the old empire of the Mauryas to settle their disputes. Thus India was saved for sixteen centuries from Western domination by the insane inability to refrain from disputes, which beset Alexander's successors like a fatal and insidious disease. "The fiercely-fighting Greeks," we are told in the Gargi-Sanhitta, "did not stay long in Madhyadesha; there was a cruel war in their own land between themselves."

The permanent power of Menander probably never extended far east of Mathura; after a long and glorious reign he died during the prosecution of some campaign, but whether in making war upon his turbulent neighbours or his Indian rivals, we are not informed. The death of the king was the signal for the sub-division of his empire among a host of petty princes, whose eagerness for the possession of his remains testifies to the disruptive powers already at work. Menander may have died shortly after Mithridates, *i. e.*, between 135-130 B. C.

After his death the Sako-Parthian kingdom, which, in the days of Menander, had been pushed back within very narrow bounds, began to grow in power, profiting, no doubt, by the dissensions among the Greeks. The accession of Mithridates II and the recovery of part of Arachosia, may have caused the Saka principalities to put themselves under Parthian protection, but ultimately an independent Saka kingdom was established, with its capital at Taxila, but having in its suzerainty another settlement whose capital was at Mathura. This conquest must have taken place after the death of Menander; and is possibly coincident with the loss of Taxila and part of the Kabul valley by the Greeks. Strato II appears to have been the last king to have ruled in the Kabul. The gradual shrinking of the Greek settlements was due partly to the drain of continual war, but even more to the process of gradual absorption. The coins of the later rulers of the Punjab show clearly that the Greek spirit was declining rapidly, as all traces of originality of inspiration or fineness of execution are gradually lost. In the meantime events had been taking place in the old kingdom of Bactria, which were destined to have a profound effect upon the fortunes of India. Two centuries of civilized life had wrought great changes among the barbarian conquerors. The Kuei-Shuang, or Kushan tribe, had conquered the other four principalities, and had embraced the Buddhist religion, and being now an organized power who had reached a considerable degree of civilization, they found little difficulty in over-running the Kabul valley. This happened between the years 50—60 A.D. and neither the degenerate Greeks, nor the once powerful Parthians, weakened by intestinal warfare, could resist the invader. The enterprising Kozulo-Kadphises does not appear to have used physical force in overcoming his (so-called) Greek opponents. Hermaeus, the last of the race, appears after the death of his wife, Calliope, to have associated Kadphises with him on his throne; on his death, Kadphises assumed sole sovereignty, and Greek rule in India was over for ever.

APPENDIX TO CHAPTER VI.

MENANDER-MILINDA.

THE authorities for Menander are fully given by V. A. Smith, pp. 192-194, 'Early History of India'.

I have also referred to Von Gutschmidt's Encyclopædia article, to Gardner's introduction to the B. M. Catalogue, and to Rhys Davids' edition of the "Questions" (S. B. E., vols. 35-36.). The question of the identity of Menander and Milinda is fully discussed by the latter. I have not here gone into it.

CHAPTER VII.

THE EFFECTS OF THE GREEK OCCUPATION.

"Ferrum victorem cepit et artes—
Intulit agresti . . . . ."

FOR over three centuries Greek rule exerted an influence, to a greater or less degree, in Northern India. What effect had this upon the development of Aryan Civilization in and around the "Middle Land"?

Did Hellenic ideals, Hellenic philosophy, art, and literature permeate the intellectual life of the East as it has done that of the West, or did India regard Alexander, Eucratides, and Menander as great conquerors merely, not as apostles of Hellenism—barbarians whose ideas were as impure and impossible to the Brahman mind as their persons in the Brahman dwelling-place? Did India simply endure Greek influence with the 'patient, deep disdain' with which she had temporarily submitted to, and ultimately overcome, so many foreign invaders?

While it is easy grossly to exaggerate the influence of the West upon the East, as Niese and others have done, it would be impossible to conceive that the settlement of Bactrian-Greeks in the Punjab left no stamp upon India during two centuries of occupation; and even when they had disappeared as a political force, the modification of the parent stock, by the admixture of the alien race which it had absorbed into its own blood, must have been fruitful of some material results. India, it is true, with her immemorial religion and literature, has never been very ready to learn from the West, which she has always considered to be somewhat contemptible, the product of a day; on the other hand, the influence of Greece was felt in India at a time of great importance in the literary and political development of the country, when it was most likely to have a strong and lasting effect.

Alexander's brilliant but ruthless descent through the Kabul Pass compelled the peoples of the Punjab, and even of Central India, to recognize the existence of a great Western power. Alexander's death was the signal for a general reaction, which swept out all traces of the Greek occupation. It did not, however, erect once more the barrier between East and West, which Alexander had shattered for ever, and henceforward, whether as enemies or as friends, conquerors or subjects, the two great civilizations were engaged in mutually borrowing ideas and principles which had been separately evolved by either.

It was not in vain that Chandragupta remembered with pride that he had seen the great conqueror face to face as a youth; this was the Ideal which inspired him to overthrow the dissolute Nanda kings, and to knit together the petty princedoms of the Ganges valley into a strong, organized empire, capable not only of stamping out every trace of the hated intruder in the Punjab, but of finally bringing Seleucus himself to his feet. Chandragupta, it is true, held "India for the Indians," against all comers, especially the Greek from the West; but it was surely the great example of Alexander who inspired India with the Ideal of the *Chakkavatti Raja*, the "King of Kings," which the Mauryas so nobly tried to realize. This being the case, we cannot say that Alexander's influence upon India is a negligible factor in the history of her development. It is not without significant meaning that we read how Chandragupta paid homage to the Altars which the Macedonian had built, ere he turned back for ever on the banks of the Hyphasis.

Once established, Greek intercourse with India by no means came to an end with the great national reaction under the Mauryas. The very fact that Megasthenes was for years an Ambassador at Pataliputra, is a significant indication of the cordial relations existing between the two races. The exchange of Indian drugs for Greek wine and figs, the naive request of Chandragupta that his imperial brother would oblige him with "a Greek sophist" are only trifling surviving records of what must have been a regular and constant intercourse between the races. It should not be forgotten that one of the first of Asoka's cares was to send messengers to preach the Glad Tidings to the dwellers in the outer darkness, his fellow monarchs of the Yavanas. The very presence of the Greeks in Bactria, the great mart where East and West met to exchange their wares, must have in itself exercised an enormous influence on both sides alike.

It is as useless to ignore the effects of Alexander's stupendous personality, in a country where personality is supremely influential, as it is to shut the eyes to the fact that Chandragupta worshipped at the Greek king's altars, or married a Greek Princess. A recent writer has held that Chandragupta did not need Alexander's example to teach him what empire meant; that the titles current in his court were borrowed from the older and more stately Persian Empire and not from the Greeks at all. If the title of satrap is here referred to, it is certainly true that it was used at all periods by the Saka Rajahs, but linguistic is not political influence, and it was the Macedonian that India deified, as she has deified many a hero whose blows she has felt, and whom she has admired in consequence, up to the days when John Nicholson stepped to his place in the somewhat vague and extensive Hindu pantheon.

In the department of literature, we should not be led to expect that Greece exercised any profound influence upon the East, as there is no reason to suppose that Bactrian invaders of the Punjab produced any literature of their own. The danger of such hasty generalizations is shown, however, when we come to examine the history of the Sanskrit drama. While it is difficult to hold, as many authorities would have us do, that the Indian drama owes its origin entirely to the West, we may well believe that it was due to the stimulus of Greek intercourse that its subsequent development is, to a great extent, due. The ancient Indian drama, as the Sanskrit word *nataka* (from *nata* "a dancer") implies, probably arose from some primitive pantomimic performances resembling those of the pre-

Thespian days of primitive Hellas, but it may well be the case that contact with the West stimulated the development of the indigenous product, and finally enabled India to produce a Kalidasa.

In mathematics, the influence of Greece was not appreciably felt, owing to the high degree of proficiency which that science had already attained independently; indeed, in this respect, the West appears to have been the debtor, for the Arabians of the Middle Ages acknowledged that they owed much to Indian learning. In astronomy, on the other hand, new life was infused into the study by the Yavanas, whom the Indian writers acknowledge to have been their instructors: here, however, the influence appears to have been Alexandrian rather than Bactrian, as the names given to two out of the five *Siddhantas*, or systems, seem to show. The *Paulisa Siddhanta* is supposed to be based on the works of Paul of Alexandria, whose date is fixed, by a reference in his own writings, about the year 378 A. D., when the great Gupta kings were ruling in the Ganges valley.

But it is by their wonderful influence upon Indian Art that the Bactrian Greeks will ever be known, and deservedly known to the world. We have already noticed the magnificent series of coins which was struck in the Punjab and Kabul during the period of Greek occupation; it remains to give some account of the still more striking sculptures of the Gandhara district, where the successors of Praxiteles, with the true versatility of the Greek, applied the graces of Greek art for the representation of the story of the Buddha. This, the last achievement of the Bactrian Greeks, and undeniably the greatest, dates from the period when their political rule was extinct, or well-nigh extinct; and the partial absorption of the race was probably necessary before the Greek mind could assimilate itself sufficiently to Eastern thought, to produce what has been admirably described as "the union of Buddhist matter and Greek form."

During the troubled time when the Greeks from Bactria, "the viciously valiant Yavanas," were engaged in carving out new kingdoms to replace those from which the barbarians had driven them; when a continuous intestine war was daily decreasing their numbers, while the power of the Sakas was threatening them in the north, it was not to be supposed that their external influence would be great. Men fighting for their existence do not produce great artistic achievements; and we are left to admire the sufficiently exquisite coins, which are the only production of this period which have survived to our days.

If the 'Questions of Milinda' may be regarded as something more than a mere romance, we have abundant evidence that Menander revived at Sagala all the traditions of the Greek City State. No Greek remains, which can, with certainty, be assigned to that period are now left, but that does not prove that there were none to survive; and art of the Indo-Greek period may well have combined the architectural excellences of East and West.

In the later and more settled times of the great Saka princes, Greek art was encouraged extensively, and its extreme purity and peculiarly Hellenic stamp, effectually prevents us from considering it to be simply the product of late cosmopolitan influence. More probably, the Greek artists, who had had little opportunity of exhibiting their skill during the fitful fever of Indo-Greek rule in the Punjab, found an opportunity and a motive in the peaceful period that followed, and the religious revival to which a powerful and orderly rule allows the requisite scope. No one, who has visited the Museums of Calcutta or Lahore, or who has travelled in the Gandhara district, or admired the bas-reliefs in the Guide's Mess at Peshawar, can fail to be struck with the extraordinary brilliance of this, the latest development of Hellenic influence.

For the Græco-Buddhist remains are not the work of mere mechanic sculptors, hired by a native monarch to lend an air of refinement to the viharas, stupas or monasteries which he had endowed. The friezes of the Gandhara district are as much the product of artists imbued with the spirit of their work as the friezes which once beautified the Parthenon. Just as in the later Bactrian coins we find Indian influence galvanizing the old Hellenic spirit into new fantastic forms of life, so in the sculptured work we behold classic feeling for proportion and restraint, modifying the exuberance of the Indian chisel, but receiving from it, in turn, a warmth and love of variety and complexity. The very monsters and demi-gods of Hellos appear in attitudes of adoration before the great spirit of the East. The admirable illustrations in Dr. A. Foucher's "L'art Græco-Bouddhique du Gandhara" (Vol. I.) form perhaps the most suitable text from which to illustrate the subject. A reference to the sculptures there depicted will readily reveal the peculiar characteristics of this school of art, and furnish conclusive proof that it is not a mere degenerate imitation of classic models.

Sometimes the friezes wear a purely Greek appearance, with Bacchanals (appropriate enough to the birthplace of Bacchus, and the region of Mount Nysa), demi-gods, dolphins. But this seems to be a mere accident; the Indo-Greek sculptor is no mere slave of classic forms; he uses them at times, it is true, but generally, merely, because they suit the panel that has to be filled. On the other hand, the sculptures are full of observations of surrounding Indian life, as they are of artistic force and freedom from convention. While the artist seems bent on showing us how Hellenic and Eastern subjects can be, the details of foliage, of costume, and of ornament, reveal that he is at heart an Indian, expressing Indian ideas through Greek modes.

Among the purely Hellenic subjects, it is interesting to notice the popularity of marine monsters and deities, perhaps owing to the proximity of the mighty Indus, which the Greeks appear, to have looked upon as something more than a river. Poseidon, it will be remembered, figures upon the coins of Antimachus, who must have regarded him as a river and not a sea-god.

A remarkable triangular panel in the Lahore Museum represents a Triton fighting with a god.

The artist evidently challenges comparison here with the Pergamene sculptures, but his work, though equally forcible and life-like, is of a perfectly independent and original type. The marine god is delineated as ending in a curling, serpent-like body, and not in the two serpent-legs of the Pergamene friezes. In another similar Triton group, on the other hand, serpent-legs appear, recalling in a curious way the coin of Hippostratus (Gard. Pl. XIV, 6, page 160). The similarities in conception in the coins of the Bactrian Greeks and the Gandhara sculptures are not without significance.

The influence of Greek art upon the architecture of the period :from the early fragment of an Iong pillar found at Matthura to the regular Indo Corinthian architecture of the second century A. D. is only one degree less noteworthy ; it shows the same originality, the same capacity for independent development along Greek lines, the same richness in inspiration, but it appears to be more directly the product of cosmopolitan influence,—more Roman than Bactrian. Perhaps Roman architecture owes something to the influence of this Indo-Greek school, for the introduction of figures among the foliage of the Corinthian capital, first found in the remains of the Baths of Caracalla (217 A. D.) in Rome, appear quite often in Gandhara pillars. The East, too, may have been responsible for the introduction of a less desirable innovation, the use of mortar and plaster to obtain meretricious effects, not attainable by the use of the chisel unaided.

It is hardly possible to conclude more fitly than by drawing attention to the supreme merit which M. Fouchet has noticed as predominant in the Bactrio-Indian bas-reliefs. "Above all," he remarks, "I must call attention to the remarkable *chastity* of the Græco-Buddhistic school of art." This is the last tribute one would be prepared to pay, not only to decadent Greek art generally but also to a great deal of Indian art. No higher tribute than this could be paid to the serious taste of the sculptors, the sincere austerity of their subjects, and the purity of their ideals.